Answer
Me
This!

Answer Me This!

Patrick Madrid

Our Sunday Visitor Publishing Division
Our Sunday Visitor, Inc.
Huntington, Indiana 46750

Our Sunday Visitor Publishing Division
Our Sunday Visitor, Inc.
200 Noll Plaza
Huntington, IN 46750

ISBN: 978-1-931709-58-3 (Inventory No. T35)

LCCN: 2003110881

Cover design by Tyler Ottinger
Interior design by Sherri L. Hoffman

PRINTED IN THE UNITED STATES OF AMERICA

To Sister Judith Zuñiga, O.C.D.,
my dear friend and sister in Christ,
with fraternal affection and *tres cosas*.

"God does not deign to save his people by means of dialectics. The kingdom of God is in the simplicity of faith, not in contentious words."

— St. Ambrose of Milan
Exposition of the Christian Faith
(Book I, chapter 5)

CONTENTS

Introduction   9

Answers to Common Questions and Objections   19

  Apologetics — *Questions* 1-2   21
  Catholicism — *Questions* 3-6   25
  Scripture Alone? — *Questions* 7-13   37
  The True Church? — *Questions* 14-15   63
  Salvation? — *Questions* 16-19   85
  The Papacy — *Questions* 20-23   105
  The Holy Spirit — *Question* 24   122
  Sacred Tradition — *Question* 25   127
  Statues, Icons, and the Sin of Idolatry —
    Questions 26-27   129
  The Blessed Virgin Mary — *Questions* 28-36   134
  The Saints — *Question* 37   167
  The Magisterium — *Questions* 38-39   169
  Books of the Bible — *Question* 40   174
  Calling Priests "Father" — *Question* 41   178
  Baptism — *Questions* 42-43   182
  Confession of Sins — *Question* 44   188
  The Eucharist — *Questions* 45-46   195
  Purgatory — *Questions* 47-48   199
  The Rapture — *Question* 49   208
  Hell — *Question* 50   218

Endnotes   221

Recommended Reading   245

About the Author   249

INTRODUCTION

An Apologist Does Not Apologize

I am a Catholic apologist, which means I do my best to provide factual, convincing answers to people's questions about Catholicism. This book of Catholic apologetics is designed to show you how to do the same thing: to answer, calmly, charitably, and effectively, many of the tough questions people these days level at Catholics.

Just to clarify, an apologist is not someone who goes around apologizing for being Catholic, as if to express regret for this or that aspect of the Catholic religion. In modern usage, the ancient word "apology" (Greek and Latin: *apologia*) has come to mean an expression of dismay or regret for something we wish hadn't happened. But originally, the meaning was exactly the opposite. An apologist is someone who offers a reasoned defense for Christianity, usually using three tools: Scripture, the facts of Christian history, and logic. "Apologetics," therefore, is the activity of presenting that defense.

The title of this book — Answer Me This! — points us to the heart of a particular challenge the Catholic Church has faced in each of the last twenty centuries (future centuries will be no different). There are many

9

competing ideologies, religions, movements, and "isms" out there, and all of them, in one way or another, raise questions, objections, and challenges to the True Faith.

To hear someone say, "Answer me this!" about some aspect of the Catholic Church and its teachings requires a choice on your part. Either you can ignore the question and walk away leaving it unanswered, or you can respond the way St. Peter exhorts us to in situations like this:

> Always be prepared to make a defense to any one who calls you to account for the hope that is in you, yet do it with gentleness and reverence. (1 Peter 3:15)[1]

"To make a defense," as St. Peter puts it, is precisely what apologetics is all about. It doesn't mean being defensive or argumentative. Rather, it means giving reasons — good, solid reasons, backed up by the evidence of Scripture, Christian history, and common sense — when questions arise, as they inevitably will. And this is nothing new in the life of the Church.

Defending the Faith — A Primer

Apologists and apologetics have been active in the life of the Catholic Church all the way back to the time of the early Christians. St. Paul was certainly one of the greatest apologists the Church has ever known. His New Testament writings in defense of Christianity against the criticisms and arguments raised by his fellow Jews, form a major portion of ancient Catholic apologetics.

In subsequent generations, the mission of the Church was assisted and fortified by apologist saints such as Justin Martyr, Irenaeus of Lyons, Athanasius, Cyprian of Carthage, Ambrose of Milan, Augustine, Jerome, and Cyril of Jerusalem, just to name a few. These and many other early Catholics came to the defense of the Catholic Church during times of controversy and persecution. Their efforts to explain and defend Catholic teaching paved the way for future generations, including our own, to safely navigate the waters of societal upheaval, theological uncertainty, persecution, and doctrinal controversies.

Later generations saw formidable apologists emerge in times of crisis and upheaval. The Middle Ages saw the rise of such giants as St. John Damascene, and later St. Bernard of Clairvaux and St. Thomas Aquinas took on the challenges of their day, dispatching objections with clarity and charity, showing from Scripture and history the truth of Catholic teaching. These men, in turn, were followed by successive waves of apologists who drew on the wide and deep reservoir of apologetics created by their forerunners.

When the Protestant Reformation began to gain traction in Europe, Catholic apologists entered the fray: St. Robert Bellarmine, St. Edmund Campion, St. Peter Canisius, and others, who engaged and refuted the

Protestant theologians with a rigorous knowledge of the Bible and the writings of the early Church Fathers.

St. Ignatius of Loyola founded the Society of Jesus, known commonly as the Jesuits, to act as a coordinated cadre of "shock troops" who would stand up for Christ and the Church in locations where either or both were under attack. In the five centuries since Martin Luther ignited the conflagration of division and theological anarchy within Christendom, Catholic apologetics has played a vital role in the communal life of the Church and in the lives of individual Christians.

Modern Challenges to the Faith

Today, apologetics is enjoying a strong and rapid revival after decades of being considered passé and, oddly, "pre-Vatican II." It's odd, because those who claim that apologetics (i.e., defending the Faith) belies an unacceptable "pre-Vatican-II" retrograde mentality, seem to have not read the documents of the Second Vatican Council very carefully.

In several places, the Council exhorts Catholics, lay people in particular, to be ready and willing to defend the truths of the Catholic Faith. For example:

> Since, in our own times, new problems are arising and very serious errors are circulating which tend to undermine the foundations of religion, the moral order, and human society itself,

this sacred synod earnestly exhorts laymen — each according to his own gifts of intelligence and learning — to be more diligent in *doing what they can to explain, defend, and properly apply* Christian principles to the problems of our era in accordance with the mind of the Church.[2]

It is quite unbecoming for the Church's children idly to permit the message of salvation to be thwarted or impeded. . . . Therefore, this sacred Synod advises them of the obligation they have to maintain and assist Catholic newspapers, periodicals and film projects, radio and television programs and stations, whose principal objective *is to spread and defend the truth* and foster Christian influence in human society.[3]

There are now, more than ever, many distinct challenges to Christ and His Church. Many voices clamor for our attention and belief. Not only are there literally thousands of Protestant denominations today, each of which ardently proclaims that it has the truth, taken straight from the Bible; there are innumerable quasi-Christian and non-Christian groups working hard to gain converts. Mormons, Jehovah's Witnesses, Seventh-Day Adventists, and Moonies, are out there in force proselytizing on the airwaves, through magazines and television commercials and, of course, through the time-tested method of going door-to-door in search of new members. No doubt, you yourself have been visited at your home at least once by a pair of smiling missionaries from the local church of (insert the name of the group here). They want to leave you their literature, start a "Bible study" with you in your home, or in some other way get you to abandon your Catholic Faith and embrace theirs.

As if that weren't bad enough, one can't turn on the radio or television without coming across Evangelical and fundamentalist broadcasts that combine good preaching with bad theology. That's a devastating combination because many Catholics these days are poorly catechized and don't really know their Faith as well as they should. For many, this is not their own fault, as they were raised at a time when, in many American and Canadian parishes, there had been little or no emphasis on teaching children the basics of Catholic teaching. Consequently, many adult Catholics today are prime targets for Protestant groups, Mormons, Jehovah's Witnesses, and other aggressive proselytizing groups.

The pews of the Protestant churches in your own town are filled with ex-Catholics. Many of the ministers preaching in those pulpits are former Catholics. This sad phenomenon is also true of your local Jehovah's Witness Kingdom Hall and the LDS stake center down the road. The next time Jehovah's Witnesses or Mormon missionaries come to your door, ask if they are converts to their religion. Invariably, you'll find that at least one will be a former Catholic.

Accepting the Challenge

So what can we do about this challenge? The first and most important thing is to not grow discouraged. After all, Christ promised:

> "I have said this to you, that in me you may have peace. In the world you have tribulation; but be of good cheer, I have overcome the world." (John 16:33)

Second, we must pray that God will imbue the Church, and each of us, with greater graces and a deeper resolve to know our Faith better and to share it more effectively with those around us. Pray, too, for the people you know who need God's grace of illumination to show them the truth.

And third, learn how to engage in Catholic apologetics. This book will provide you with basic answers you can give when questions and challenges come your way. There are also many other good books out there (see the recommended reading list at the end of this book), as well as programs on EWTN and your local Catholic radio station that will enhance your ability to explain and defend the Faith. The key thing to remember is that apologetics should always be a labor of love, never haughty or condescending. We must each approach our non-Catholic or former-Catholic friends or neighbors in a spirit of humility and charity. This book will show you what you can say in response to questions that come up, but I must emphasize here that *how* you respond is even more important than what you say. Charity and patience, when combined with solid biblical and historical evidence, are the most potent and effective tools you can use in your efforts to explain and defend the Faith.

I know this to be true, partly as a result of my own failings as an apologist and in the times when I wasn't charitable or patient in dealing with a non-Catholic's objections (you see, like everyone else, I need to take this advice to heart, too). More important, though, are those examples given to us by the great apologist saints, not only by what they wrote or preached in defense of the Faith, but by their charity in dealing with opponents. We can follow their example and that of St. Paul, who warned Timothy about entering into foolish debates with others and reminded him:

> The Lord's servant must not be quarrelsome but kindly to every one, an apt teacher, forbearing, correcting his opponents with gentleness. God may perhaps grant that they will repent and come to know the truth, and they may escape from the snare of the devil, after being captured by him to do his will. (2 Tm 2:24-26)

Everyone Has Questions

My own experience over the years has shown me the truth of St. Paul's words. Since the late 1980s, I've been privileged to conduct apologetics seminars at hundreds of Catholic parishes, universities, and other venues across the country and abroad. One thing is the same wherever I have spoken, whether to audiences of fifty or five thousand: people out there have lots of questions about the Catholic Church. Sometimes folks will pose their questions politely, sometimes not. Often, deep emotions such as anger, resentment, suspicion, and fear bubble beneath the surface in the hearts of those who lash out against the Catholic Church with objections to its doctrines. The only way to help answer them, I have found, is to be patient and kind, as St. Paul said.

In the course of conducting hundreds of parish apologetics seminars, I've fielded literally thousands of pointed questions about and objections to the Catholic Church, its doctrines and customs, its history, and its stance on controversial moral issues such as contraception, abortion, euthanasia, in vitro fertilization, cloning, and homosexuality. Catholics and non-Catholics alike want solid, convincing answers to these questions, and we owe them that. My hope is that this apologetics book will help you help them.

ANSWER ME THIS!

Answers to Common Questions
and Objections

1. The term Catholic "apologetics" just doesn't make sense to me. I know it means "defending the Faith," so why not just say defending the Faith? Don't you think "apologetics" sounds like you're apologizing for being Catholic?

A wag once quipped that "Apologetics means never having to say you're sorry." It's a cute saying (especially if you're familiar with the 1970s movie line it's spoofing) that highlights the linguistic problem you bring up.

You're right. These days, the word "apologetics" does have the connotation of being sorry for something. And while it's true that many people these days think apologetics means to regret something, the original and longstanding meaning of the word is to "give a defense" for something, to provide a reasoned explanation when faced with a question or an objection. As St. Peter said in 2 Peter 3:15: "Always be prepared to make a defense to any one who calls you to account for the hope that is in you, yet do it with gentleness and reverence." The underlying Greek is: "*hetoimoi de aei pros apologian*," which means "give an answer," or "give a defense." As you can see, the word "apologetics" derives from the Greek word St. Peter used: *apologian*.[4] It's in this sense that we use the word "apologetics."

One good reason for not relying solely on the phrase "defending the Faith" when you mean apologetics is the likelihood of some interpreting that to mean "being defensive" or "combative" when engaged in apologetics. And nothing could be further from the authentic meaning of apologetics. Carried out correctly and according to the mind of Christ and the Church, apologetics should always be conducted with charity and respect, never in a defensive or haughty way (cf. 2 Tim. 2:24-25).

Rather than abandon the rich vocabulary of the Bible and the last two thousand years of Catholic Tradition to accommodate modern sensibilities, it's a far better thing, in my view, to recover the use of this excellent term. Indeed, even within the last twenty years, we've seen a dramatic increase in awareness among lay people and clergy alike of the importance of apologetics in the life of the Church. Along with this resurgence has come a renewed and ever more widespread common use of the word apologetics, according to its authentic meaning. I suspect (and hope!) that within another twenty years or so, the phrase "Catholic apologetics" will no longer sound odd to anyone. It will be so much a part of mainstream Catholic vocabulary that no one will get the wrong impression.

2. **Why must you apologists (Catholic and Protestant) endlessly debate these religious issues all the time? All the apologetics debates, articles, books, tapes, and videos you people keep cranking out con-**

tain nothing new that hasn't been argued about hundreds of times. Why bother?

You're correct that doctrinal issues have been debated repeatedly, in fact millions of times down through the ages since the time of Christ. But the mere fact that claims about doctrine are debated, and debated frequently, doesn't in the slightest mean that those doctrines aren't important or that they shouldn't be tested against the evidence.

To use a parallel example, consider the fact that there are, amazingly, some today who argue that the Nazi Holocaust against the Jews in Europe during World War II never happened. The fact is, it *did* happen, and people should never forget that it happened.[5] If we forget or deny the reality of that horrific tragedy, we become much more vulnerable to its happening again (and again, and again). You know the oft-quoted saying: "He who does not learn from history is doomed to repeat it."

Others make the insane argument that abortion (which is more accurately called infanticide, the deliberate killing of innocent unborn children) should be legal. The "pro-choice" screamers are the pathetic echo of earlier generations of misguided people who argued that human slavery should be legal, or that women should not have the right to vote, or that Blacks should not be allowed to eat at "White-only" restaurants or drink from "White-only" drinking fountains. I could go on enumerating examples of issues that are well worth debating, but I'm sure you get the point.

If five hundred years from now some are still denying the Holocaust or promoting slavery, or saying abortion should be legal, I hope those debates far in the future will be joined by those who will be willing to spend the time and energy necessary to refute those claims. Shirking one's duty to stand up for what is true is never a permissible option, and great tragedies result when good men and women say nothing and do nothing to prevent them.

So remember this: When it comes to arguments and objections raised against the teachings of Jesus Christ and the Catholic Church, it's fair to say that those issues are even more worth debating. Truth matters. And making an honest and sincere effort to locate the truth, and then embrace it, is a very good thing indeed. Christ promised, "If you continue in my word, you are truly my disciples, and you will know the truth, and the truth will make you free" (John 8:31-32). He wants us to find and embrace the truth, even if it takes struggle and work to accomplish.

Don't be troubled that the kinds of Catholic issues you'll read about in this book are debated among Catholics and non-Catholics, as they have been for the last twenty centuries. That's not going to change (unfortunately) until Christ returns and all these questions will be definitively answered, and all debates will become moot. In the meantime, let us glorify God by following His loving appeal to each one of us: "Come now, let us reason together" (Isaiah 1:18).

CATHOLICISM

3. Christianity is really about relationships, not rules, legalism, and obedience. Christ's message is one of love and relationships. Why are Catholics so hung up on rules and regulations?

It's not that Catholics are "hung up" on rules and regulations for their own sake, but rather, we recognize that Jesus Christ himself wants us to obey certain rules and regulations — namely, those He and His apostles set forth. This should be true of all Christians.

You're right, of course, that Christianity really is about relationships, in particular our relationship with Almighty God and with all the members of the Body of Christ.[6] And like any human relationship one has with a wife, husband, parents, siblings, children, coworkers, or friends, how we follow the rules of those relationships matters a great deal with regard to how happy or unhappy those relationships will be.

If you're a parent, you expect your children to obey the rules you've laid down for your household. Sure, you have a close, loving relationship with your eight-year-old son, but you also expect him to clean up his room, eat dinner with the family, take out the trash,

25

and do his homework, right? There are certain things you tell him he must do and other things — such as don't play with matches, don't tease your sister, and don't lie — are things he must not do. These, of course, are rules, and you impose those rules on your children, not because you're "hung up" on rules, but because you know those rules are good for them and, if they're followed, they'll contribute to a happy and harmonious home. In other words, the more we live by the rules, the better our relationships are. And if this is true of a human family, it's even truer of God's family, the Church.[7]

God gave the Ten Commandments to Moses about thirty-two hundred years ago. All those "thou shalts" and "thou shalt nots" were the first major set of rules set down by God, and I'm sure you'd agree that we must obey them, just as we want everyone around us to obey them, too. After all, you wouldn't want to be murdered, or lied about, or see someone lust after your wife, or have your next-door neighbor covet or even steal your possessions, would you? Of course not. Those rules are worth living by, otherwise we would have unendurable societal chaos and misery, not to mention the fact that we would be sinning against God by breaking the commandments, a path that leads inexorably to eternal misery.

The same is true about other rules the Lord has given us, such as: Give drink to the thirsty, clothe the naked, visit the imprisoned, shelter the homeless,[8] believe in Me,[9] be baptized for the remission of your sins,[10] eat My flesh and drink My blood in the Eucharist,[11] listen to the teachers I have appointed and commissioned to instruct you,[12] obey the teachings of the Church I established,[13] and so on.

There are numerous other statements Christ made about the importance of living according to the precepts He provided for us to be truly happy and truly free:

- "Why do you call me 'Lord, Lord,' and not do what I tell you?" (Luke 6:46).
- "Not every one who says to me, 'Lord, Lord,' shall enter the kingdom of heaven, but he who does the will of my Father who is in heaven" (Matt. 7:21).
- "If you would enter life, keep the commandments" (Matt. 19:17).

St. John echoes the Lord's words, saying:

Beloved, if our hearts do not condemn us, we have confidence before God; and we receive from him whatever we ask, because we keep his commandments and do what pleases him. And this is his commandment, that we should believe in the name of his Son Jesus Christ and love one another, just as he has commanded us. All who keep his commandments abide in him, and he in them. And by this we know that he abides in us, by the Spirit which he has given us. (1 John 3:21-24)

That last passage reveals the heart of the issue. By paying attention to the rules the Lord has given to His family, the Church, we are truly living out our relationship with Him and with one another, as He desires us to. That is the best and happiest kind of relationship with Him we could possibly want.

4. The New Testament doesn't say anything about a "Catholic" Church. It says in Acts 11:26 that the disciples of Christ were called "Christians," not "Catholics." Where did the moniker "Catholic" come from?

It's true that the New Testament doesn't contain the word "Catholic," just as it doesn't contain the word "Trinity," which is a term accepted by all Christians. But this is reflective of the fact that the early Church had not yet been able to develop the sophisticated theological vocabulary we enjoy today. Also, it didn't take long after the time of the Lord's public ministry before heretical Christians,[14] described by St. Paul as "fierce wolves," would create factions and divisions among the faithful (cf. Acts 20:29-32).

With the various factions that arose in those early days, it became difficult at times for the faithful to discern who was a "fierce wolf" preaching heresy and who was a fellow orthodox believer. After all, many of the rivals went under the name Christian as well. And so, quickly and naturally, a term arose that could not be misunderstood as a description of the Church to which the true disciples of the Lord belonged. The name "Catholic" arose very early to serve that need.

It comes from the Greek compound word *katholokos*, derived from the word *katholou*, meaning "for the whole" (*kathos* plus *holos*). Although we don't know when, where, or by whom the term "Catholic" first began to be used as the formal name for the Church, we do know that it had become part of the common usage among Christians at least by the beginning of the second century. For example, in one of his epistles[15] St. Ignatius of Antioch matter-of-factly referred to the Church as the "Catholic Church."

The theological implications of the term Catholic can be glimpsed in Matthew 28:19-20, where Christ commissioned the Church to "Go therefore and make disciples of all nations." Thus, the word Catholic conveyed the identity and mission of the Church very handily. Its mission is for all people, in all places, at all times.

Around the year A.D. 345, the great Eastern Church Father St. Cyril of Jerusalem commented on the meaning and importance of the name "Catholic":

"And if ever thou art sojourning in any city, inquire not simply where the 'Lord's house' is — for the sects of the profane also attempt to call their own dens, 'houses of the Lord' — nor merely where the 'church' is, but where is the Catholic Church. For this is the peculiar name of the holy body the mother of us all. . . . Now it [the Church] is called Catholic because it is throughout the world, from one end of the earth to the other."[16]

The truth is, even though the early Church progressed from referring to itself in the more generic form of "Christian" to the more specific "Catholic," it remained one and the same Church with all the same teachings, Traditions, Scriptures, and ministry.

5. Jesus didn't come to start a "church" or a religion; He came to bring us the gospel of salvation. The Catholic Church is all about man-made religion, not the Gospel.

Actually, the Bible is clear that the Lord intended to do both: establish a Church and bring us the gospel of salvation. And as the old song says, you can't have one without the other. In fact, these two things are inextricably connected. Christ established the Church to be the means by which His Gospel would be preached to all the nations, baptizing and teaching with His own authority.[17] St. Paul said:

> To me, though I am the very least of all the saints, this grace was given, to preach to the Gentiles the unsearchable riches of Christ, and to make all men see what is the plan of the mystery hidden for ages in God who created all things; that *through the church* the manifold wisdom of God might now be made known to the principalities and powers in the heavenly places. (Eph. 3:8-10)

It is in and through this one Church He established that He wants all men to be reconciled to the Father through himself. It is completely alien to Scripture, indeed to the Gospel message itself, to attempt to separate the Church and the Gospel.

Passages such as these make it quite clear that Jesus did indeed establish a Church and that His followers understood this:

> "And I tell you, you are Peter, and on this rock I will build my church, and the powers of death shall not prevail against it." (Matt. 16:18)

> "If your brother sins against you, go and tell him his fault, between you and him alone. If he listens to you, you have gained your brother. But if he does not listen, take one or two others along with you, that every word may be confirmed by the evidence of two or three witnesses. If he refuses to listen to them, tell it to the church; and if he refuses to listen even to the church, let him be to you as a Gentile and a tax collector. Truly, I say to you, whatever you bind on earth shall be bound in heaven, and whatever you loose on earth shall be loosed in heaven." (Matt. 18:15-18)

> So the church throughout all Judea and Galilee and Samaria had peace and was built up; and walking in the fear of the Lord and in the comfort of the Holy Spirit it [i.e., the Church] was multiplied. (Acts 9:31)

Notice the singular "church," not "churches," which points to the singular quality of the *ekklesia* the Lord had established. He did not come to initiate "Christianity" per se, an amorphous collection of like-minded believers who were not united. No. He established a particular Church that was (and is) His Body;[18] one, holy, Catholic, and apostolic.

6. **The notion that the Catholic Church could possibly be the original Church is laughable. After all, one doesn't have to look far to see evidence of horrible corruption and hypocrisy among Catholics. And I'm not just talking about the so-called "bad popes" in previous centuries. Turn on the TV news and you'll see what I'm talking about. The Bible says the real Church is the "bride of Christ," "spotless and unblemished." Catholics don't fit that description.**

This is not an unreasonable objection and, unfortunately, many today share your attitude toward the Catholic Church. While you've drawn an incorrect conclusion, I can understand what brought you to this point of view.

First, let's start by admitting that there is absolutely no excuse for the current crop of deplorable scandals within the Catholic Church, or for any scandals among Catholics of any era. The Lord himself offered this harrowing warning to those who would be the cause of grave scandal:

> "Temptations to sin are sure to come; but woe to him by whom they come! It would be better for him if a millstone were hung round his neck and he were cast into the sea, than that he should cause one of these little ones to sin." (Luke 17:1)

The first part of this passage is worth emphasizing: "Temptations to sin are sure to come." The Lord knew there would be those in the Church who would become the source of scandal. He'll punish them in due time if they don't repent and amend their lives, of course, but note that He didn't say that His Church would be free from such miserable characters. (And as you say, one need only turn on the television news or read the local paper to see examples of what He meant.)

Also, keep in mind that in the parable of the "Wheat and the Weeds," Christ foretold that His Church would contain good and bad, saint and sinner (Matt. 13:24-43).

In that parable, the Church is in the world, not of it, and as Christ said, the good and bad members (the wheat and weeds) will coexist side by side until the Last Day. Christ's intention has never been to remove all possibility of sin and failure ("I do not pray that thou shouldst take them out of the world, but that thou shouldst keep them from the evil one" [John 17:15]). He knew that there would be "weeds" alongside the "wheat" in His Church.[19] And we have seen this truth played out in every age since the days the Lord walked the earth during His public ministry.

To use an analogy that will help make this point, let's take the situation of a world-class cardiologist who is a renowned expert in the area of heart disease. When he gives medical advice, you know you can trust it because he has the experience, the years of research, and the facts of science to back up his opinions. By anyone's estimation, he's not just a cardiology expert, he's an authority. Nevertheless, let's say he himself lives like a slob, eating nothing but fatty fast food, never exercises, drinks like a fish, is massively overweight, and chain-smokes.

It's the classic case of someone who knows better but doesn't act on it.[20] He doesn't live according to what he knows to be true (i.e., that chain-smoking, drinking too much alcohol, not exercising, being obese, and cramming a steady diet of greasy, fatty hamburgers into your mouth will eventually kill you). But this physician's own personal lack of discipline, which we can rightfully criticize, doesn't change by a fraction the fact that he is a medical authority on heart disease. This is a helpful if imperfect analogy because it shows us a parallel to the problem of bad Catholics.

The fact that there are unrepentant and hypocritical sinners in the Catholic Church, mixed in among those who are striving to be holy and faithful to God's grace and live as best they can according to His commandments, does not in any way negate the truth of the Church or its teachings. The truth of the Catholic religion is either proved or disproved on its own biblical and historical merits, not on the basis of the greater or lesser degrees of sinfulness or virtue among its members.

If you don't believe that's true, here's something else for you to ponder. Christ himself handpicked twelve men to be His inner circle, His apostles, His closest friends and collaborators. And yet we see that even these handpicked men were sinful and at times even wicked.

Judas betrayed Christ, later falling into the sin of despair and committed suicide.[21] Simon Peter denied the Lord three times,[22] once under oath. All of the apostles, with the exception of St. John, ran away in cowardice and deserted their master when His hour had come and danger and death engulfed Him.[23] I think it's reasonable to assert that by any standard of measurement, those were terrible, scandalous sins. And even before those dark days of the Passion, we read plenty of examples of sinfulness on the part of the apostles: quarreling among themselves over status, pride, hard-heartedness, boastfulness, etc. Now realize that in spite of these chosen ones' personal sinfulness, Christ was still able to use them for a great mission. While this fact is a sign of contradiction in the eyes of men,[24] in God's eyes it is a manifestation of His grace and power.

Keep in mind that regardless of Simon Peter's grievous sin of denying the Lord three times, God's grace was more powerful than his sin. Peter repented of his sin, and he was restored to grace.[25] And as we know, the Bible and Christian history tell us that he went on to preach inspired teaching,[26] receive divine revelation,[27] deliver binding doctrinal decisions and teachings for the Church at the Council of Jerusalem,[28] and compose two epistles of inspired inerrant Scripture.[29]

The Lord's plan for His Church will not be thwarted by its sinful members.[30] If the sinful behavior of the members of his Church could do that, then Christ was either a liar or a fool for saying in Matthew 16:18-19 that He would build His Church on a rock and that nothing, *not even the gates of hell*, could overcome it.[31] The Church still has the authority and mission He entrusted to it even if unworthy popes, bishops, priests, Religious, and lay people, through their own sinfulness and weakness, fall by the way. God's grace is more powerful than man's sin.

And as a final point to consider, recall that God was willing to use a murderer (Moses)[32] and an adulterer *and* murderer (King David)[33] to teach His people and write inspired Scripture. In spite of their sinfulness, those men repented of their sins and went on to do great things for the Lord. This same principle is still at work in the Church. Even though some, perhaps many, of those Catholic "hypocrites" you mentioned may never repent of their wickedness, some will, and for that we give glory to God.

You see, in the end, the Catholic Church is not merely a human enterprise. It's a divine institution comprised of human members. The Catholic Church is "owned and operated" by Jesus Christ. And this means that the mission and authority of the Church doesn't derive from its members. Nor does the behavior of its members, good or bad, cause the Church to lose her mission and authority given to her by Christ. He will fulfill His promise to perpetually guide and protect His Church,[34] even from its own sinful members.

Left to ourselves, Catholics would have destroyed the Church centuries ago. But this is Christ's Church, not ours. And as He said, "With men it is impossible, but not with God; for all things are possible with God" (Mark 10:27).

SCRIPTURE ALONE?

7.   As a Bible-believing Christian, I worship the Lord in "spirit and truth" not, as Catholics do, according to human traditions that "void the word of God" (Matt. 15:6). You need to abandon all your man-made traditions and read your Bible!

I appreciate your encouragement to read the Bible. At least we can agree on how important that is. My reading of the Bible has shown me two things that are pertinent to your comment.

First, reading the Bible carefully over the years, and comparing what it says with how the earliest Christians understood it, I've discovered that if anything qualifies as a tradition of men that "voids the Word of God," it is the Protestant notion of *sola scriptura* that you are espousing here. The theological principle of going by the Bible alone, is itself nowhere taught in the Bible. And this is the fatal flaw of this Protestant theory. For in order for the idea of Scripture being the sole, sufficient rule of faith to be a coherent, workable proposition (i.e., I will only accept those teachings I can find in the Bible and I therefore will reject any teaching that I cannot find in the Bible), it must itself be somewhere expressed in Scripture or it is nothing more than a self-refuting proposition.

The fact is, the notion of the Bible being the sole, sufficient rule of faith is nowhere present in the Bible, either implicitly or explicitly, in a single passage or in an amalgamation of passages. It just isn't there anywhere in the Bible.[35]

But guess what *is* in the Bible: the teaching that we are to embrace Tradition, those Traditions that come from God himself. In fact, the Bible specifically prohibits us from going by the Bible alone in an attempt to ignore those Traditions that come down to us outside the pages of Scripture:

> So then, brethren, stand firm and hold to the traditions which you were taught by us, either by word of mouth or by letter. (2 Thes. 2:15)

> Be imitators of me, as I am of Christ. I commend you because you remember me in everything and maintain the traditions even as I have delivered them to you. (I Cor. 11:1-2)

In these passages the word "tradition" is used, from the same root word for tradition in Greek (*paradosis*). This is the same word as is used in Mark 7:1-3 and Matthew 15: 1-9. The difference is that in the former verses, "tradition" is good and necessary and, by the way, unwritten (i.e., not in the Bible), while the latter verses show an example of a tradition of human origin that conflicts with God's revelation and, therefore, must be abandoned.[36]

The Protestant doctrine of *sola scriptura* is one such doctrine. It voids the Word of God because it falsely reduces "the Word of God" to just the written Word of God. St. Luke makes it clear that the teachings of Christ and the apostles were transmitted to later generations of Christians both through the written word (e.g., the New Testament Gospels and epistles) and also through oral teaching and preaching in the life of the Church:

> Inasmuch as many have undertaken to compile a narrative of the things which have been accomplished among us, just as they were delivered to us by those who from the beginning were eyewitnesses and ministers of the word, it seemed good to me also, having followed all

things closely for some time past, to write an orderly account for you, most excellent Theophilus, that you may know the truth concerning the things of which you have been informed. (Luke 1:1-4)

8. You claim that the Protestant doctrine of *sola scriptura* is "not in the Bible," but 2 Timothy 3:16-17 clearly teaches the sufficiency of Scripture.

Sorry. No dice. 2 Timothy 3:16-17 can't help you vindicate *sola scriptura*. A Protestant apologist I debated some years ago discovered this fact to his chagrin and discomfiture (which was all the more discomfiting because it took place in front of an audience that had been eagerly anticipating his never-delivered promise to furnish proof of the Bible's sufficiency from the Bible itself).[37] Let's quote the passage he tried to use in his attempt to make his case for *sola scriptura* and see if it contains any trace of *sola scriptura*:

But as for you, continue in what you have learned and have firmly believed, knowing from whom you learned it and how from childhood you have been acquainted with the sacred writings which are able to instruct you for salvation through faith in Christ Jesus. All scripture is inspired by God and profitable for teaching, for reproof, for correction, and for training in righteousness, [so] that the

man of God may be complete, equipped for every
good work. (2 Tim. 3:14-17)

In this passage, notice that St. Paul reminds his young
protégé, Timothy, that "All scripture is inspired by God
and is useful for teaching, for refutation, for correction,
and for training in righteousness, [so] that the man of
God may be competent, equipped for every good work."

The conclusion Protestants want to draw from this
passage is that because St. Paul says that all Scripture is
inspired by God and that Scripture can make the man
of God "competent" and "equipped for every good
work," that this somehow means that these statements,
therefore, entail the conclusion that Scripture is sufficient. For several important reasons, that conclusion is
simply not warranted; indeed it can be conclusively ruled
out by the internal evidence of this passage.

First, notice that the Greek phrase for "all Scripture is inspired" is "*pasa graphé theopneustos.*"[38] This
literally means "each" or "every" Scripture is inspired
by God. This complicates matters for Protestants, because if St. Paul were, in fact, implying the idea of the
sufficiency of Scripture in this passage, he is designat-
ing *each individual book* of Sacred Scripture as sufficient in itself for the tasks he goes on to outline. But
that, of course, is not what Paul is saying here.

Second, notice that the particular Scriptures St. Paul
refers to are those Scriptures that Timothy had learned
"from childhood." So, if this statement proves *sola scrip-*

tura, it proves way too much for the comfort level of Protestants. For it would mean that the Old Testament Scriptures are sufficient in themselves, to the exclusion of the New Testament, for the tasks that the "man of God" will accomplish that St. Paul outlines in verses 16-17. I doubt any Protestants would want to make that claim.

Third, notice that nowhere in this passage do we see even the slightest mention (or implication) that the Bible is the sole sufficient rule of faith. Indeed, a few passages earlier in this same epistle, St. Paul wrote:

> What you have *heard* from me, keep as a pattern of a sound teaching, with faith and love in Christ Jesus.[39]

Then, a few sentences later, he adds:

> You then, my son, be strong in the grace that is in Christ Jesus. And *the things you have heard me say in the presence of many witnesses* entrust to reliable men who will also be qualified to teach others.[40]

As you can see, the norm St. Paul wants Timothy to go by is not Scripture alone, but also the oral teaching he delivered to Timothy personally and through others. This oral teaching, the faithful and accurate handing down of the Gospel of Christ in the Church,[41] which includes the correct interpretation of the Scriptures, is Sacred Tradition.[42]

What's more, in 2 Timothy 2:15, St. Paul exhorts Timothy to "rightly divide the word of truth." Many

Protestants assume that the phrase "word of truth" is a synonym for "the Bible." But this is not true. The phrase "the word of truth" is not restricted just to Scripture; it also extends to oral tradition. Two examples of this are Ephesians 1:13 and Colossians 1:5, where "the word of truth" refers specifically to apostolic Tradition, not to Scripture.

What all this shows us is that St. Paul, far from asserting that Scripture is sufficient in an absolute sense, intended for Timothy (indeed, all Christians) to make use of Scripture and Tradition in conjunction with the teaching authority of the magisterium of the Church. After all, St. Paul himself was among the original bishops, the original magisterium. We see here that St. Paul didn't simply tell Timothy to become the best Bible student he could. He emphasized that Timothy had to learn how to correctly understand and teach the authentic meaning of Scripture.[43] This dovetails perfectly with St. Peter's warning about those who are "ignorant" of how to correctly interpret the Bible:

> There are some things in them [i.e., the writings of St. Paul] hard to understand, which the ignorant[44] and unstable twist to their own destruction, as they do the other scriptures. (2 Peter 3:16)

Third, we have to examine the alleged implication of Scriptural sufficiency drawn from the statement that Scripture will make the man of God "complete" and "equipped for every good work." Does this comment indicate that St. Paul believed that the Bible was sufficient apart from Tradition and the magisterium of the Church?[45] Not at all.

During that debate with the Protestant apologist I mentioned earlier ("Does the Bible Teach *Sola Scriptura*?"), he attempted to make his case for *sola scriptura* by using what he must have thought was a clever analogy of a bike shop. It may have been clever, but it completely backfired on him.

The Protestant apologist argued that just as a bicycle shop would stock all the necessary equipment for bike-riding enthusiasts, in the same way the Bible is sufficient to "fully equip" the man of God. Unfortunately, for his case, that analogy, although superficially plausible, falls apart, and the audience saw it straight away.

I pointed out that although a bike shop might indeed be able to furnish all the necessary equipment for bike riding, the customer must first know how to ride a bike, or all that shiny new equipment won't do him any good. This, I said, is analogous to a Christian knowing how to correctly interpret Scripture (remember what St. Peter said about those who are untrained and can't accurately interpret Scripture!). The fact is, a bike shop can equip someone with the finest bicycle and the best cycling equipment money can buy, but it doesn't teach him how to ride the bicycle.

The Protestant debater attempted to skirt around this fact by countering that 2 Timothy 3:17 says the "man of God" is specifically the one under discussion in this passage, not some anonymous person. He felt that it meant that there is no doubt that a man of God would know how to use Scripture correctly. This argument backfired, too, because there was no way for him to determine for sure who is a "man of God" and who isn't. As I wrote in an article:[46]

> Protestantism is so divided over central doctrinal issues (e.g., infant baptism, baptismal regeneration, the nature of justification, salvation, divorce and remarriage, etc.), that this "man of God" argument only begs the question. All Protestants believe that they've embraced the "correct" interpretation of Scripture, but doing so includes the implicit assertion that all the other denominations don't have the correct interpretation on all things. If they did, why the need for denominations? The answer to the Protestant claims of formal sufficiency in this passage is that Paul is not trying to establish Scripture as the sole, sufficient thing that renders the man of God fit for these tasks. Rather, he is reminding Timothy of several things that, combined with God's grace and Timothy's faithful diligence, will make him so equipped.

> There's also the lexical argument based on the Greek of 2 Timothy which argues that because Scripture will make the man of God "*artios*" (suitable) and "*exartizo*" (thoroughly furnished), it therefore is sufficient. But this argument fails for several reasons.

First, with regard to what Scripture says about itself, 2 Timothy 3:16-17 merely says that Scripture is *ophelimos*, which means "useful" or "profitable." Paul's use of the Greek terms *artios* ("suitable" or "correct") and *exartismenos* ("having been furnished") does not imply the sufficiency of Scripture, on purely lexical grounds. Although some Greek scholars note that *artios* and *exartizo* could mean sufficient, we must do our best to understand their actual meaning based on the context of this passage.

A telling fact is that no major Bible translation, not even those produced by the most ardent supporters of *sola scriptura*, renders either *artios* or *exartismenos* into English as "sufficient." Furthermore, the "sufficiency" hermeneutic Protestants use in 2 Timothy 3:16-17 fails when applied to similar passages.

For example, in 2 Timothy 2:19-21, Paul exhorts Timothy to cleanse himself from all that is not holy and virtuous, saying that doing so will make him "ready for any good work" (verse 21). The exact same Greek phrase is used here as in 2 Timothy 3:16: *pan ergon agathon* ("for every good work"). Under the "sufficiency" hermeneutic used by Protestants to defend *sola scriptura* in 2 Timothy 3:16, Paul would here be made to say that one's personal efforts to become purified from sin are "sufficient." But, of course, that would be an absurd conclusion.

We can see the same absurdity in the Protestant argument arise when it's applied to James 1:4: "And let steadfastness have its full effect, that you may be perfect (*teleion*) and complete (*holoklepoi*), lacking in nothing (en *medeni leipomenoi*)." This passage uses far stronger language than that found in 2 Timothy 3:16-17, and goes far beyond the mere implication of sufficiency Protestants want to see in this verse, by the explicit statement that perseverance will make you "perfect and complete, lacking in nothing."

If any verse in the Bible could be used to argue for "sufficiency" James 1:4 would be it. Under the hermeneutic employed by the proponents of *sola scriptura*, in this passage James would be saying that all one needs is perseverance (the context is perseverance in suffering and good works!). This would mean that mere perseverance is sufficient, and such things as faith, grace, prayer, repentance, even Scripture, are unnecessary. Again, an absurd proposition, but that's what this form of Protestant argumentation leads to, not only here in James 1:4, but also in 2 Timothy 3:16-17.

Some Protestants wind up committing a lexical fallacy in their attempt to ward off the obvious implication of James 1:4 and 2 Timothy 2:19-21. They claim that, because the word *teleios* is used in James 1, not *artios*, the two passages cannot be compared. But the fact is, the primary meaning of *teleios* is "complete," or "perfect." It's a much more forceful word for indicating perfection or completion than is *artios*, which primarily means merely "suitable" or "fit."[47] And if the *artios/exartizo* argument proves anything, it proves too much. 2 Timothy 3:16-17 shows that *artios* and *exartizo* modify "the man of God" (*ho tou theou anthropos*), not "Scripture" (*graphé*). The simple fact is that Scripture does not claim sufficiency for itself here. It says it completes and makes fit the man of God. So, at best, this argument could only prove that Scripture makes the man of God sufficient.

9. **The Catholic Church misrepresents the testimony of the Church Fathers on the sufficiency of Scripture! They definitely taught *sola scriptura*. For example, St. Basil of Caesarea wrote: "Therefore, let God-inspired Scripture decide between us; and on whichever side be found doctrines in harmony with the Word of God, in favor of that side will be cast the vote of truth" (*Epistle ad Eustathiu*).**

The Catholic Church does not misrepresent the Church Fathers, rather, it let's them speak for themselves without prejudice. If you pluck statements out of the Fathers' writings, here and there, and without consideration for the totality and continuity of their thought, you can make it appear that they said one thing or another in a way that would be contrary to what they really meant. Jehovah's Witnesses and Mormons (and, sadly, some Protestant apologists) are skilled at this "cut and paste" form of quoting the Church Fathers.

So, let's see what St. Basil really meant by his statement that you quoted. First, you'll have to think again if you think the above statement from St. Basil must mean that this great Catholic bishop and doctor of the Church would have been comfortable with this classic Protestant expression of *sola scriptura*:

> All things in Scripture are not alike plain in themselves, nor alike clear unto all; yet those things which are necessary to be known, believed, and observed, for salvation, are so clearly propounded and opened in some place of Scripture or other, that not only the learned, but the unlearned, in a due use of the ordinary means, may attain unto a sufficient understanding of them.[48]

Catholics could respond to that bit of illogic saying, "Can you point to even one example in the Bible or Christian history of Scripture 'interpreting itself'?" (The answer, of course, will be no.) "And how exactly does the Bible 'decide' which passages are clear and which are unclear? What form does that take? After all, the meaning of passages such as Matthew 16:18-19 and John 6:22-69 seem very clear to Catholics." The fact is, the Bible can't interpret itself, but the Church established by Christ can, and for the fifteen centuries prior to the Protestant Reformation, the historic Christian Church consistently believed and taught the Catholic model of authority,[49] not *sola scriptura*.

There is no doubt, based on the evidence in his other writings, that the great Catholic bishop St. Basil of Caesarea would have recoiled in horror from that Protestant formulation of *sola scriptura*. Survey his writings and you'll see that he held Scripture high as the written standard of truth in the Church (which is why he challenged his Bible-quoting opponent in the statement above to let Scripture decide between them), but he in no way denied the authority of Sacred Tradition, which is the portion of the body of teaching that comes to us from Christ and the apostles (i.e., the "Deposit of Faith") through the lived understanding of the Church, outside the pages of Scripture. Here are two powerful examples of St. Basil's teaching on this subject that should put to rest any lingering doubt that he did not believe or teach the Protestant notion of *sola scriptura*:

> Of the beliefs and practices whether generally accepted or enjoined which are preserved in the Church, some we possess derived from written teaching; others we have delivered to us in a mystery by the apostles by the tradition of the apostles; *and both of these in relation to true religion have the same force.* (*On the Holy Spirit*, 27)

In answer to the objection that the doxology in the form with the Spirit has no written authority, we maintain that if there is not another instance of that which is unwritten, then this must not be received [as authoritative]. But if the great number of our mysteries are admitted into our constitution without written authority [i.e., of Scripture], then, in company with many others, let us receive this one. For I hold it apostolic to abide by the unwritten traditions. "I praise you," it is said[50] "that you remember me in all things and keep the traditions just as I handed them on to you," and, "Hold fast to the traditions that you were taught whether by an oral statement or by a letter of ours."[51] One of these traditions is the practice which is now before us [under consideration], which they who ordained from the beginning, rooted firmly in the churches, delivering it to their successors, and its use through long custom advances pace by pace with time. (*On the Holy Spirit*, 71)

Those two passages from the writings of St. Basil, among the many others that could be adduced here, suffice to demonstrate that the holy bishop in no way believed or taught the Protestant theory of *sola scriptura*. The same is true for the other early Fathers. My advice to Protestants on this issue is: Read the Fathers in their totality to understand their real views. Picking quotes out of context is an art form that's been perfected by Jehovah's Witnesses and others. Avoid that mistake.

And to Catholics I say, don't become flustered when someone challenges you with a quote from this or that early Church Father that seems to prove a Protestant teaching. The early Church Fathers were Catholic and, as we showed above with St. Basil, a bit of digging into their writings will show this, time after time.[52]

10. Look at these two quotes from the early Church Father St. Athanasius: "The holy and inspired Scriptures are sufficient of themselves for the preaching of the truth" (*Contra Gentiles*, 1:1), and, "These books [of canonical Scripture] are the fountains of salvation, so that he who thirsts may be satisfied with the oracles contained in them. In these alone the school of piety preaches the Gospel. Let no man add to these or take away from them" (*39th Festal Letter*). How can you deny that he taught *sola scriptura*?

It's easy. As we saw in the previous chapter, the totality of St. Athanasius' writings quickly reveals that he didn't teach *sola scriptura* in the sense that you, as an Evangelical Protestant, assert it. This great Catholic bishop and defender of Trinitarian orthodoxy might appear here to be promoting a "Bible only" view in these quotes, but he really was not. For example, close examination of his *39th Festal Letter* shows that St. Athanasius was providing liturgical guidelines for the priests and deacons in the churches of his diocese regarding what was permitted to be read at Mass as Scripture.[53] In some locales, non-canonical Christian writings were sometimes read during the eucharistic liturgy alongside the New Testament Gospels and epistles, and St. Athanasius was here putting a stop to that, saying that only those canonical books were allowed to be read as Scripture.

And we can dispense with the myth that St. Athanasius was a *sola scriptura* man — he wasn't — by looking at a few other comments he made on this issue:

"The confession [i.e., the formal teachings] arrived at Nicea[54] was, we say more, sufficient and enough by itself for the subversion of all irreligious heresy and for the security and furtherance of the doctrine of the Church" (*Ad Afros*, 1).

"[T]he very tradition, teaching, and faith of the Catholic Church from the beginning was preached by the apostles and preserved by the Fathers. On this the Church was founded; and if anyone departs from this, he neither is nor any longer ought to be called a Christian" (*Ad Serapion*, 1:28).

Can there be any doubt left that St. Athanasius was definitely no friend of the Protestant teaching of *sola scriptura*? I don't think so. And what's more, since many Protestants quote him out of context, rightly thinking him to be an authority worthy of giving important advice, I'd advise everyone to think carefully and prayerfully about this great saint's warning that one who departs from Catholic Tradition "neither is nor any longer ought to be called a Christian."

11. Okay. You won't be able to get around this passage from the writings of St. Cyril of Jerusalem. In it, he clearly teaches the doctrine of *sola scriptura*. Not even Houdini could wiggle out of this proof from the early Church in favor of the sufficiency of Scripture: "In regard to the divine and holy mysteries of the Faith, not the least part may be handed on without the Holy Scriptures. Do not be led astray by winning words and clever arguments. Even to me, who tell you these things, do not give ready belief, unless you receive from the Holy Scriptures the proof of the things which I announce. The salvation which we believe is not proved from clever reasoning, but from the Holy Scriptures" (*Catechetical Lectures*, 4:17).

Actually, I don't need to be Houdini to answer this one because there's no wiggling or squirming involved to show that St. Cyril did not here or elsewhere teach the doctrine of *sola scriptura*.

This statement is not problematic for Catholic teaching on the authority of Scripture and Tradition, but it is, ironically, highly problematic for Protestants who want to press this Church Father into service in an attempt to prove he believed in the sufficiency of Scripture. In fact, as a Protestant believes in *sola scrip-*

tura, you face a major dilemma with only two options, neither of which I think you will like.

Option One: If St. Cyril of Jerusalem was, in fact, teaching the idea of the sufficiency of Scripture here in *Catechetical Lectures* (or in any of his other writings, for that matter), how do you account for the fact that the *Catechetical Lectures* are filled with his vigorous teachings on such peculiarly Catholic doctrines as the infallible teaching office of the Catholic Church (18:23), the Mass as a sacrifice (23:6-8), the concept of purgatory and the efficacy of expiatory prayers for the dead (23:10), the Real Presence of Christ in the Eucharist (19:7; 21:3; 22:1-9), the theology of sacraments (1:3), the intercession of the saints (23:9), holy orders (23:2), the importance of frequent Communion (23:23), and baptismal regeneration (1:1-3; 3:10-12; 21:3-4), indeed a staggering array of specifically Catholic doctrines and practices?[55]

These are the very same Catholic doctrines that Fundamentalists and Evangelical Protestants claim are not found in Scripture. So, the problem is that if St. Cyril really held to the notion of *sola scriptura*, then you'd have to accept the fact that he also believed he had found those Catholic doctrines in the Bible. You would then be forced to conclude that he was badly mistaken in his exegesis of Scripture. But you can immediately see that this conclusion is devastating to the Protestant position, because it would instantly impugn any credibility that St. Cyril might have had as a trustworthy biblical exegete. And if he has no credibility as an interpreter of the Bible, because he claimed to find all those other doctrines in the Bible (i.e., all those Catholic ones that Protestants argue are unbiblical), then how can he be credible as an authority on finding *sola scriptura* in the Bible? Obviously, he couldn't be.

Now for Option Two: St. Cyril did not teach *sola scriptura*; the Protestant understanding of the passage you quoted is simply incorrect because it is out of context. That means that any attempt to cite that quote in support of *sola scriptura* would be futile (if not dishonest), because it would require a hopelessly incorrect understanding of St. Cyril's method of systematic theology, the doctrinal schema he sets forth in *Catechetical Lectures*, and his overall view of the authority of Scripture and Tradition.

Obviously, neither of these two options would be palatable to a Protestant who wants to see in St. Cyril of Jerusalem a champion of *sola scriptura*. The simple fact is, St. Cyril was a faithful Catholic bishop who, like St. Athanasius and St. Basil, would have rejected the Protestant notion of the absolute sufficiency of the Bible, bereft of Sacred Tradition and the teaching authority of the magisterium of the Catholic Church.

12. The pastor of the nondenominational church I attend preached a sermon last Sunday in which he said that, during the Middle Ages, the Catholic Church kept all the Bibles "chained up" so that people wouldn't have access to the Word of God. Is that true?

Yes, it is true, but not for the reason your pastor claimed. Keep in mind that, during the many centuries between the writing of the various books of the Old and New Testaments until the invention of the printing press in the 15th century,[56] each copy of Sacred Scripture, whether in scrolls or in book form, was extremely precious to Christians. This was because of the relative scarcity of copies, which meant that great care was taken to preserve these copies in churches, monasteries, convents, universities, and other places where copies of the Bible might be found.

During the Middle Ages, we see throughout Europe, as well as in parts of North Africa and Asia Minor, the rise of monastic orders dedicated to the study of God's written Word. One of the great services rendered by these monks was that they hand copied biblical manuscripts, often spending years painstakingly transcribing the parchment scrolls so that future generations of Christians would have access to them. It was very common in those days for parts of the Bible to be "illuminated" with precious metal, such as gold leaf, and with elaborate and beautiful calligraphy letters and drawings, all done to glorify God and draw the heart of the reader of Scripture heavenward.

As these exquisite volumes of Scripture were brought forth for use in the community, it was only natural that the local church or monastery that owned them would take steps to ensure they were not stolen. One of the most common ways to do this was to attach a chain to the binding of the Bible. In churches across Europe, one could routinely find Bibles chained to the pulpit. But as you can see, the reason was hardly sinister. They were chained, not to keep them away from people, but for precisely the opposite reason: so that they would be available for the people, which wouldn't be possible if they had been stolen.

So, yes, the Catholic Church did chain Bibles in the past. And, as has been pointed out before, it did so for the same reason the telephone company chains telephone books in phone booths: so that they'll be there when you want to use one.

13. Is it true that the Catholic Church burned Bibles to prevent people from discovering the truth?

Yes and no. Yes, at times Catholics have burned Bibles, but for understandable reasons, as we'll see in a moment. And no, the Catholic Church never burned Bibles in an effort to keep people in the dark about what the Bible says. By the way, an interesting aspect of this issue is that, while Protestants are typically the ones who level this charge against the Catholic Church, Protestants were themselves responsible for quite a bit of Bible-burning. (Somehow, though, that historical fact never seems to be brought up.)

First, let's see why Catholics sometimes burned Bibles. In each case, you'll find that this action was taken to prevent the spread of error among the faithful from heretical versions that omitted passages, added spurious passages, altered the words of Scripture, or included misleading or outright incorrect footnotes that would confuse the reader and lead him away from biblical truth. We can safely assume that no sincere Christian would tolerate such defects in his or her personal Bible, and it's just as true that the Catholic Church would not do so either.

Here's a real-world, modern-day example of this issue: the Jehovah's Witnesses *New World Translation of the Bible*. This seemingly benign version of Scripture is riddled with serious problems. In an effort to twist the meaning of the biblical text to better conform to the Watchtower's aberrant theology, the Jehovah's Witnesses who prepared this defective edition of the Bible deliberately inserted words into certain passages that do not belong there, and they mistranslated words and phrases in an effort to prop up their beliefs.

Perhaps the most notorious example of this deception appears in John 1:1, where the Jehovah's Witnesses added the indefinite article "a" in the English: "In the beginning was the Word, and the Word was with God, and the Word was a god" (New World Translation). The insertion of this article is both grammatically incorrect and intentionally misleading because it leads the unsuspecting and untaught Bible student to the erroneous conclusion that Christ, the "Word" spoken of here (cf. John 1:14), was not God himself, as Catholics and all other Christians believe, but merely "a god." Another example of this defect involves the dozens of instances where the Greek word for "Lord' (*kurios*) is routinely mistranslated as "Jehovah." In Hebrews 2:13 and Revelation 4:8, the Greek word for "God," *theos*, is mistranslated as "Jehovah."

A myriad of examples of this sort of deceptive tampering with Scripture by Jehovah's Witnesses could be cited to show how those who crafted the New World Translation systematically manipulated and mistranslated the Bible in an attempt to obscure its authentic meaning, distorting it enough to make it appear to agree with their errors.

Clearly, these grave defects would be (and have been) injurious to the faith of anyone who comes into contact with them. And that presents a good argument for eliminating such corrupted versions of the Bible if one was in a position to legally do so.

Unlike today, in centuries past, especially in Europe, the Catholic Church *was* in a position legally to prevent defective versions of the Bible to wreak spiritual and theological havoc among the faithful. So, when the Church became aware of the existence of such Bibles, it wisely had them burned to prevent them from causing harm. The Church did not, however, burn any Bible out of a desire to prevent the faithful from knowing what was in the Bible. That accusation is completely baseless.

To use an analogy, let's say that after a particularly unhygienic person visited your home, you discovered that the bed in your guestroom was infested with fleas. Next you discovered that simply washing the sheets doesn't get rid of the pests. In fact, just carrying the flea-ridden sheets to the laundry room would spread the fleas throughout the rest of your house (not to mention the fact that you would have them all over you!).

What would you do in that situation? Most likely you'd simply get rid of the sheets, taking them straight to the garbage can. Or you might even *burn* them — anything to make sure the sheets couldn't spread their cargo of fleas. You'd do this to protect yourself and the rest of your family, not because you hate bed sheets and don't want your family to know the joys of sleeping on smooth linen. Right? Of course.

Well, that's exactly why the Catholic Church sometimes burned defective Bibles: to prevent the spread of contagious error. Ask yourself this question: Given that the Catholic Church, in her monasteries and universities, labored diligently during centuries between the apostolic age and the invention of the printing press to preserve, perpetuate, and propagate the Bible throughout all parts of the known world, does it really make sense to you that the Catholic Church would then go around burning Bibles? Of course not. Over the course of history, the Holy Bible has had no greater champion and defender than the Catholic Church. Just keep in mind that a thousand years before Martin Luther was even a twinkle in his daddy's eye, the Bible was being painstakingly hand-copied and distributed throughout Christendom by untold numbers of Catholic monks, nuns, and lay scholars who loved Sacred Scripture and spent their lives toiling to ensure that future generations of Christians would have the Bible.

And let's not forget that our Protestant friends have a history of Bible-burning in their past, too. For example, the Protestant reformer John Calvin, a self-proclaimed lover of the Bible, didn't care for the version of Scripture that a Protestant rival of his, Michael Servetus, had released, so he did not hesitate to order them confiscated and burned. (Not content with that, when Calvin was eventually able to have Servetus arrested, he had *him* burned, too.)[57]

After King Henry VIII[58] abandoned the Catholic Church and set himself up as the head of his new Protestant enterprise, the Church of England ordered the wholesale burning of all Catholic Bibles and other religious writings in churches, convents, and monasteries across the realm, including in Ireland.[59] During this phase of his madness, anyone found in possession of a Catholic Bible was punished by death. Queen Elizabeth I[60] followed his murderous policy against Catholics in 1582 by mandating the burning of Catholic Bibles, especially the Catholic Rheims edition of the New Testament in English, which had just been released.

For decades, printing *any* Bible in English was illegal in England. Only the King James Bible could be printed, and then only by printers authorized by the government. All other Protestant Bible versions discovered by the authorities were confiscated and destroyed. One humorous episode of Protestant Bible-burning involved an edition of the King James Bible itself. In 1631, an edition of the King James Bible was printed and someone goofed in the typesetting stage. Exodus 20:14 was found to be missing the word "not." Which changed the commandment to "Thou shalt commit adultery," which, as you might imagine, caused some commotion among Protestants of the day. Needless to say, the King of England, Charles I, ordered those Bibles to be burned.[61]

In 1653, another slipup at the printer occurred; the word "not" was again omitted, and 1 Corinthians 6:9 was printed as an eyebrow-raising, "Know ye not that the unrighteous shall inherit the kingdom of God?" This edition, too, was consigned to the flames. In 1702, the King James Bible suffered yet another indignity when a hapless typesetter mistakenly printed Psalm 119:161, which should read, "Princes have persecuted me," to read instead: "Printers have persecuted me."

Need we say more?

THE TRUE CHURCH?

14. Why is the Pope of Rome wasting so much time and energy trying to bring about reunion between the Catholics and Orthodox? The Orthodox Church

has its own rituals, customs, and doctrines, and they're happy. Why can't he respect the fact that they are separate and different from the Catholic Church?

The Pope is absolutely doing the right thing by seeking unity with the Orthodox. It's tragic to see the stubborn, proud resistance he often faces from some in the Orthodox world, who are antagonistic to the very thought of unity with the Catholic Church. But Jesus Christ wants nothing less than unity for His flock: "And I have other sheep, that are not of this fold; I must bring them also, and they will heed my voice. So there shall be one flock, one shepherd" (John 10:16). A few chapters later, in John 17:17-23, the Lord prayed earnestly that His followers all be one, as He and the Father are one.

In light of those passages in which Christ makes it clear how important it is to Him that there be unity among His followers, we should deplore the disunity that exists between Orthodox and Catholics (not to mention Protestants). The Pope does more than just deplore it; he's working in every way he can to help heal it. Unfortunately, the problem of disunity he's working to correct is as old as the hills.

The tendency toward schism and discord among Christians was, sadly, present even among those who lived at the time of the apostles. St. Paul warned against this when he wrote: "I appeal to you, brethren, by the name of our Lord Jesus Christ, that all of you agree and that there be no dissensions among you, but that you be united in the same mind and the same judgment. For it has been reported to me by Chlo'e's people that there is quarreling among you, my brethren. What I mean is that each one of you says, 'I belong to Paul,' or 'I belong to Apol'los,' or 'I belong to Cephas,' or 'I belong to Christ'" (1 Cor. 1:10-13).

Those who criticize the Pope's efforts for unity with the Orthodox should ask themselves these questions: Isn't it an unbiblical, even *anti*-biblical, attitude to refuse to seek the unity that St. Paul commands us to seek? Or are we free to disregard St. Paul's exhortation? Is it not merely wrongheaded but actually deeply contrary to a spirit of fraternal charity, indeed to the very Gospel of Christ itself, to stubbornly refuse to work for a resolution of the rift between the Orthodox peoples and the Catholic Church? I believe the answers to these questions are clear.

Second, in Matthew 18:17, Jesus explained how to resolve ecclesiastical problems: "If he refuses to listen to them, tell it to the church; and if he refuses to listen *even to the church*, let him be to you as a Gentile and a tax collector." In the early centuries of Christianity, when the people of what would today be known as the Orthodox Churches were in full communion with the Catholic Church, it was understood that to be in communion with the bishop of Rome, the pope, was the single most important criterion for claiming to be "in the Church."

Given that Orthodoxy is a loose confederation of autonomous and autocephalous churches (i.e., not one single "Church" per se), how could one actually follow the Lord's directive in this passage? To which of the many Orthodox Churches would he turn to? The Russian Orthodox? The Orthodox Church in America? The Greek Orthodox Church? What about the Armenian Orthodox or the Orthodox Church of Albania?[62] How would you know which of them, if any, to turn to, since they're all fiercely independent of one another?

And third, let's recognize that both the Orthodox Churches and the Catholic Church agree that they have a common heritage, valid sacraments, and that they were united, even if imperfectly, prior to the definitive split in the year 1054. So that means that the Orthodox once were in union with the Catholic Church and in communion with the pope as the vicar of Christ.[63] So, if Christ desires unity for His flock, which once was united, why shouldn't the Pope work to regain that unity once more? Indeed, why shouldn't all Catholics and Orthodox of good will follow the Pope's example and work for the unity Christ desires for us?

15. **What makes you so sure the Catholic Church is the true Church and all others are not? Surely you don't think that people in other denominations aren't Christians?**

Without doubt, there are many sincere and devout Christians within Protestantism. The Catholic Church recognizes Protestants as Christians, but she also sees that they have an incomplete Christianity that is to greater or lesser extents, depending on the denomination, distorted by the inclusion of various errors (e.g., traditions of men that nullify the Word of God,[64] such as *sola scriptura* and *sola fide* [Latin: justification by faith alone]), and by the omission of certain authentic Christian doctrines (e.g., the rejection of the sacraments, especially the Eucharist, and the denial of doctrines such as baptismal regeneration, the intercession of the saints in heaven, and the existence of purgatory). Even though these Christians have, without realizing it, an imperfect and incomplete form of Christianity, there is no doubt that untold numbers of them are sincerely seeking to know, love, and serve Jesus Christ, and for that we give thanks to God.

The real question is, in spite of one's sincerity and heartfelt desire to serve the Lord, what are the objective evidences we can examine that can help us discover which of all the Christian groups out there, including the Catholic Church, contains the "fullness" of Christianity that Christ wants us all to have? Or to say it a different way, in spite of one's sincerity, how can we know, of all the Churches, which is the one, true Church established by Jesus Christ?

There are many compelling biblical and historical reasons for being sure that the Catholic Church[65] is the Church established by Jesus Christ. The evidence that supports this conclusion is powerful and over-whelming.

Before we briefly examine that evidence, let me first offer a word of caution. We must keep in mind that simply because one can conclude with certitude, based on the facts, that the Catholic Church is the one, true Church established by Christ, that doesn't give a license to any Catholic to feel personally superior to non-Catholics. Haughtiness, triumphalism, and condescension have no place in the heart of one who recognizes the truth and embraces it. As we consider the reasons why people can be sure the Catholic Church is what it claims to be, we can't lose sight of the fact that our ability to perceive this truth is a gift of God, not something we take credit for. And most importantly, this is a gift that God wants us to strive to share with those around us. That means we have to always work to cultivate a spirit of friendliness, charity, and *humility* in the ways we share the truth with others (cf. 2 Tim. 2:24-25).

Direct-marketing gurus have for years stressed the cardinal rule for successful mailings: "Test, test, test!" What they mean is, don't leave to chance something as important as spending your hard-earned marketing budget. They tell you to test the different possible ways of writing and packaging an envelope — the color, content, etc. — all in an effort to find out which combination works best. Once they find the winning combination, marketers can then spend their money wisely and expect good results.

NASA won't send a rocket into space without first performing huge numbers of tests to make sure its equipment and calculations are all in order. Ditto for plane manufacturers. The airlines won't buy a new jet, much less fill it with passengers and let it take off, unless it has been rigorously tested ahead of time to ensure quality and safety. This approach is part of practically every area of life.

This same axiom, "Test, test, test!" applies to you and me, too. And here, in the area of discerning religious truth, the need to be sure we have the right information is infinitely more important than spending our money. So it's with this in mind that I invite you to test what I am about to offer you by way of evidence that the Catholic Church is the Church established by Christ. You can test it in various ways, the most important three ways being: check Scripture, check the writings of the early Christians, also known as the early Church Fathers and Councils, and check your own motives and prejudices (we all have them) through prayer. Ask God the Holy Spirit to guide and illuminate you with His grace. And then, as you make a sincere and prayerful effort to sift and discern, think of these important words of St. Paul: "Test everything; hold fast [to] what is good" (1 Thes. 5:21). Wise words, indeed.

Let's take a backward glance across the last twenty centuries of Christian history in search of evidence that can help us discern whether the Catholic Church can rightly claim to be the one, true Church.

Her claim is that, alone among all other Churches, the Catholic Church can demonstrate both its continuous existence since the time of Christ (no other Church can do this), as well as a continuity in its teachings. We can see the Catholic Church alive and well in each of the last twenty centuries since the time of Christ and the apostles, and at any given point in history you might examine, you will find those specifically Catholic doctrines being taught.

And when you think about it, this must be so. The Church Christ established *must* be visible in each century, from the day it was established until the end of the world. There are three reasons why this must be so:

1) Christ said that His followers are "the light of the world. A city set on a hill cannot be hid" (Matt. 5:14). This means that the Lord didn't go to all the trouble of establishing His Church only to hide it from view, making it difficult or impossible to locate and enter. No, He imbued His Church with certain clear, recognizable characteristics. What a cruel hoaxer Christ would have been otherwise!

2) Christ said, "Nor do men light a lamp and put it under a bushel, but on a stand, and it gives life to all in the house" (Matt. 5:15). Clearly, Jesus wouldn't give us advice that He

himself wouldn't follow. Just as He wants each of us individually to let our "light shine before men" (Matt. 5:15), so, too, does He want His Church to radiate the light of His truth in all places and at all times.

3) Christ said to His infant Church, "Lo, I am with you always, to the close of the age [i.e., the end of the world]" (Matt. 28:20). This means that from that moment forward, there never would be a time when his Church didn't exist.

Here's a simple test you can conduct to verify this and test the Catholic Church's claim. Today you will find the Catholic Church around the world teaching its peculiarly Catholic teachings: the Real Presence of Christ in the Eucharist, devotion to Mary and the saints, the Mass as a holy sacrifice, the sacraments, the authority of the bishop of Rome, the existence of purgatory and the efficacy of prayers for the souls of the deceased, infant baptism, confession to a priest, the authority of Tradition, the divinity of Christ, the Trinity, the inspiration of Sacred Scripture, the Incarnation of Christ, the Atonement, the reality of a literal heaven and hell, the importance of prayer, etc.

Dial back five hundred years. You'll find the same Catholic Church — complete with the pope, bishops, and priests, and lay faithful — believing and teaching those very same peculiarly Catholic doctrines. Notice, though, that many of today's aggressively proselytizing Christian and quasi-Christian groups simply didn't exist five hundred years ago: The Mormons, Jehovah's Witnesses, Seventh-day Adventists, *Iglesia ni Cristo*, Calvary Chapel, and the myriad "non-denominational" denominations that have sprung up in the last century. In fact, once you pass beyond five hundred years, all of Protestantism disappears. The Lutheran, Reformed, and Baptistic branches of the Protestant rebellion from the historic Christian Church all vanish as we examine Christian history prior to beginning of the 16th century.[66]

Now go back another five hundred years. You'll see the religious landscape as it looked at the dawn of the second millennium. And there you will see the Catholic Church preaching and teaching those same doctrines.

Go back another five hundred years. Now you're in the Middle Ages. What Christian Church will you find unfurled gloriously throughout much of Europe, in Asia, and across all of the vast Mediterranean Basin — from Spain to Syria, from Tunisia to Egypt, from the British Isles all the way down to the Arabian Peninsula?

That's right. You'll find the capital "C" Catholic Church, complete with the pope, the seven sacraments, the Mass and the Eucharist. You'll see the Catholic Church proclaiming, believing, and defending those very same peculiarly Catholic doctrines. You'll see infant baptism, the Mass, belief in the Real Presence of Christ in the Eucharist, devotion to the Blessed Virgin Mary and the saints. You'll encounter the popes, as the bishops of Rome and successors of St. Peter, governing the Universal Church in both temporal and theological matters, sometimes skillfully, sometimes ineptly. But no one can deny the Catholic Church was that Church one finds during those centuries.

Now, cast your gaze back across the remaining few centuries, the fourth, third, second. Now you are near the end of the first century. Most of the original apostles have been martyred and gone on to glory to receive their reward. The Apostle John is now an old man in exile, but is still alive and revered by Christians. We are at the close of the Apostolic Age. And here we see the Catholic Church, teaching and proclaiming the faith in seed form, developing a new theological vocabulary on the fly, pushing outward, spreading the light of Christ and "all those things [He] has commanded" us to believe and obey.[67] The Church is still in its infancy. It doesn't yet have many of the external features and characteristics it will eventually acquire; no Vatican City, no titles like "monsignor," and no magnificent cathedrals and basilicas erected to the glory of God. Those things will come along in due time, but here, at the close of the first century, what you encounter is the primitive Church, the Church in its "mustard seed" form.

> He said therefore, "What is the kingdom of God like? And to what shall I compare it? It is like a grain of mustard seed which a man took

and sowed in his garden; and it grew and became a tree, and the birds of the air made nests in its branches." (Luke 13:18-19)

This is a crucial passage to ponder as we look at the evidence unfolding before us. We have to remember that the Church, the kingdom of God, is, like a mustard seed, an organic entity. This means it grows and develops. And just as you don't today resemble very closely how you looked when you were a one-year-old baby, even so, you are the very same person. You've grown and changed in your outward appearance over the years, but you are still the same unique individual you were back when you still wore diapers.

The same is true of the Catholic Church. As Christ himself promised, this Church would grow and eventually come to look much different than its original form. So don't let it throw you when certain external qualities of the Catholic Church today aren't visible in earlier centuries. The externals are not what's important. What *is* important is to recognize the very same entity teaching the very same doctrines, then as now. Let me give you an example of what I mean.

Look at the year A.D. 80. You'll see the bishop of Rome, Pope St. Clement I, issuing a letter of encouragement and admonition to another important diocese. In that letter he wrote these words:

> Owing to the sudden and repeated calamities and misfortunes which have befallen us, we must

acknowledge that we have been somewhat tardy in turning our attention to the matters in dispute among you, beloved, and especially that abominable and unholy sedition, alien and foreign to the elect of God, which a few rash and self-willed persons have inflamed. Accept our counsel and you will have nothing to regret. . . . If anyone disobey the things which have been said by him [the Lord] through us, let them know that they will involve themselves in transgression and in no small danger. You will afford us joy and gladness if being obedient to the things which we have written through the Holy Spirit, you will root out the wicked passion of jealousy.[68]

This is a good example of what I mean by the Church extending back in time to the first century. In the quote from St. Clement, bishop of Rome, we see one of the very first popes exercising authority in another established church. This is an example of one of those "peculiarly Catholic" doctrines — the papacy — which non-Catholics reject. And yet, here we see undeniable evidence that the Catholic teaching of the primacy of the bishop of Rome was present and visible in the very earliest years of Christianity. Here are some other examples of papal primacy in the early Church:

St. Ignatius of Antioch, circa A.D. 107-110 — "Ignatius . . . to the church also which holds the presidency, in the location of the country of the Romans, worthy of God, worthy of honor, worthy of blessing, worthy of praise, worthy of success, worthy of sanctification, and, because you hold the presidency in love, named after Christ and named after the Father. . . . You [the Church at Rome] have envied no one, but others you have taught. I desire only that what you have enjoined in your instructions may remain in force" (*Letter to the Romans,* 1:1).

St. Irenaeus of Lyons, A.D. 189 — "But since it would be too long to enumerate in such a volume as this the succession of all the churches, we shall confound all those who, in whatever manner, whether through self-satisfaction or vainglory, or through blindness and wicked opinion, assemble other than where it is proper, by pointing out here the successions of the bishops of the greatest and most ancient church known to all, founded and organized at Rome by the two most glorious apostles, Peter and Paul, that church which has the tradition and the faith which comes down to us after having been announced to men by the apostles. With that church, because of its superior origin, all the churches must agree, that is, all the faithful in the whole world, and it is in her that the faithful everywhere have maintained the apostolic tradition" (*Against Heresies,* 3:3:2).

St. Irenaeus of Lyons, A.D. 189 — "Matthew also issued among the Hebrews a written Gospel in their own language, while Peter and Paul were evangelizing in Rome and laying the foundation of the Church. . . . But since it would be too long to enumerate in such a volume as this the succession of all the churches, we shall confound all those who, in whatever manner, whether through self-satisfaction or vainglory, or through blindness and wicked opinion, assemble other than where it is proper, by pointing out here the successions of the bishops of the greatest and most ancient church known to all, founded and organized at Rome by the two most glorious apostles, Peter and Paul, that church which has the tradition and the faith which comes down to us after having been announced to men by the apostles. With that church [i.e., with Rome], because of its superior origin, all the churches must agree, that is, all the faithful in the whole world, and it is in her that the faithful everywhere have maintained the apostolic tradition" (*ibid,* 3:1:1; 3:3:2).

Consider these three representative quotes from the first and second centuries regarding the early Christian belief in the Real Presence of Christ in the Eucharist — which is another of those Catholic doctrines so hotly disputed by so many Protestants, as well as Mormons and Jehovah's Witnesses.

The Eucharist:

St. Ignatius of Antioch, circa A.D. 107 — "I have no taste for corruptible food nor for the pleasures of this life. I desire the bread of God, which is the flesh of Jesus Christ, who was of the seed of David; and for drink I desire his blood, which is love incorruptible" (*Epistle to the Romans,* 7:3).

St. Ignatius of Antioch — "Take note of those who hold heterodox opinions on the grace of Jesus Christ which has come to us, and see how contrary their opinions are to the mind of God. . . . They abstain from the Eucharist and from prayer because they do not confess that the Eucharist is the flesh of our Savior Jesus Christ, flesh which suffered for our sins and which that Father, in his goodness, raised up again. They who deny the gift of God are perishing in their disputes" *(Epistle to the Smyrneans,* 6:2-7:1*)*.

St. Justin Martyr, A.D. 151 — "We call this food Eucharist, and no one else is permitted to partake of it, except one who believes our teaching to be true and who has been washed in the washing which is for the remission of sins and for regeneration and is thereby living as Christ enjoined. For not as common bread nor common drink do we receive these; but since Jesus Christ our Savior was made incarnate by the word of God and had both flesh and blood for our salvation, so too, as we have been taught, the food which has been made into the Eucharist by the Eucharistic prayer set down by him, and by the change of which our blood and flesh is nurtured, is both the flesh and the blood of that incarnated Jesus" *(First Apology,* 66*)*.

Purgatory:

Tertullian, A.D. 216 — "A woman, after the death of her husband . . . prays for his soul and asks that he may, while waiting, find rest; and that he may share in the first resurrection. And each year, on the anniversary of his death, she offers the sacrifice" *(On Monogamy,* 10:1-2*).*

St. Cyprian of Carthage, A.D. 253 — "The strength of the truly believing remains unshaken; and with those who fear and love God with their whole heart, their integrity continues steady and strong. For to adulterers even a time of repentance is granted by us, and peace is given. Yet virginity is not therefore deficient in the Church, nor does the glorious design of continence languish through the sins of others. The Church, crowned with so many virgins, flourishes; and chastity and modesty preserve the tenor of their glory. Nor is the vigor of continence broken down because repentance and pardon are facilitated to the adulterer. It is one thing to stand for pardon, another thing to attain to glory; it is one thing, when cast into prison, not to go out thence until one has paid the uttermost farthing; another thing at once to receive the wages of faith and courage. It is one thing, tortured by long suffering for sins, to be cleansed and long purged by fire; another to have purged all sins by suffering. It is one thing, in fine, to be in suspense till the sentence of God at the day of judgment; another to be at once crowned by the Lord." *(Letter 51,* To Antonianus, 20*).*

St. Cyril of Jerusalem, A.D. 350 — "Then we make mention also of those who have already fallen asleep: first, the patriarchs, prophets, apostles, and martyrs, that through their prayers and supplications God would receive our petition; next, we make mention also of the holy fathers and bishops who have already fallen asleep, and, to put it simply, of all among us who have already fallen asleep, for we believe that it will be of very great benefit to the souls of those for whom the petition is carried up, while this holy and most solemn sacrifice is laid out" *(Catechetical Lectures, 23:5:9)*.

You will also see, if you do a bit of easy research, that these kinds of powerful and authoritative statements of early Christian belief in doctrines such as the authority of the Bishop of Rome and the Real Presence of Christ in the Eucharist could be multiplied practically endlessly with regard to the other Catholic teachings mentioned above. They are all present and visible in the early Church.[69] Why? Because the early Church was the Catholic Church.[70] Underlying all of these doctrines in the early Church is the foundational claim by innumerable early Church Fathers that the Catholic Church is the "One, True, Church."

Now let's consider what the Bible says about the identity of the Church established by Jesus Christ and how we can be sure it was indeed the Catholic Church.

A Biblical Snapshot of the Church That Christ Established

Now let's see what evidence we can briefly examine that will shed light on the nature and mission of the Church Christ established. Certainly, Bible-believing Christians of all stripes are willing to consider what the Bible can tell us about that Church. Perhaps the best way to present this case in a brief, compact form would be to examine an important passage in the New Testament that tells us a lot about the nature and characteristics of the original Church and use it as a test to see how the Catholic Church measures.

> Now the eleven disciples went to Galilee, to the mountain to which Jesus had directed them. . . . And Jesus came and said to them, "All authority in heaven and on earth has been given to me. Go therefore and make disciples of all nations, baptizing them in the name of the Father and of the Son and of the Holy Spirit, teaching them to observe all that I have commanded you; and lo, I am with you always, to the close of the age."[71] (Matt. 28:16, 18-20)

There's a vast amount of information packed into these few short words. What we see in this passage will help answer the question why one can be sure the Catholic Church is the Church Christ established and which He sent forth into the world to carry the Gospel. We can break it down into several elements.

The Authority to Go Forth in Christ's Name

Christ sent this Church (represented here by the eleven remaining apostles, the first bishops) into the world on a mission. He endowed with His conferral of authority to accomplish the mission He sets out for it. He has all authority, and with that authority He sends the Church forth. This was foretold by Christ in various places in the Gospels, for example, in Luke 10:16: "He who hears you hears me, and he who rejects you rejects me"; and John 13:20: "Truly, truly, I say to you, he who receives any one whom I send receives me; and he who receives me receives him who sent me." This means that the Church the Lord sent out that day goes forth with His authority. When we listen to and receive that Church, Jesus promises that we're listening to and receiving himself.

The implication of this part of the passage is that you and I should look for *that particular* Church, as opposed to any other, however sincere or pleasant its members may be, because only *that particular* Church was sent forth by Christ with His authority.

A Mandate to Make Disciples of All Nations

This is a key, though often overlooked, aspect of the Church that Jesus Christ established. When He said "make disciples of all nations," He was pointing to the need for all people everywhere — men, women, and children — to become disciples, *members*, of this Church. The Lord doesn't want anyone to settle for anything less than the one, true Church He had established. He wants everyone to come into that Church.

What's more, the very nature of "all nations" means that this Church has a universal mission. It's not restricted to any particular time, place, or group of people.

Sacramentality

Christ said that this Church's mission would have a distinct sacramental dimension: "Make disciples of all nations, baptizing them in the name of the Father, and of the Son, and of the Holy Spirit." This means that the normative means of bringing new converts into the Church would be through baptism. "And he said to them, 'Go into all the world and preach the gospel to the whole creation. He who believes and is baptized will be saved; but he who does not believe will be condemned' " (Mark 16:15-16).

We see this sacramental dimension even in the earliest days of the Church's ministry.[72] "Immediately upon St. Paul's conversion to Christ he was told, "The God of our fathers appointed you to know his will, to see the Just One and to hear a voice from his mouth; for you will be a witness for him to all men of what you have seen and heard. And now why do you wait? *Rise and be baptized, and wash away your sins*, calling on his name" (Acts 22:14-16).

The Authority to Teach in Christ's Name

This Church wasn't merely sent forth to preach and then move on to the next town. The Lord endowed the Church with His own authority to teach in His name:

"He who listens to you listens to me." (Luke 10:16)

"And I tell you, you are Peter, and on this rock I will build my church, and the powers of death shall not prevail against it. I will give you the keys of the kingdom of heaven, and whatever you bind on earth shall be bound in heaven, and whatever you loose on earth shall be loosed in heaven." (Matt. 16:18-19)

"Truly, I say to you, whatever you bind on earth shall be bound in heaven, and whatever you loose on earth shall be loosed in heaven." (Matt. 18:18)

Perpetuity

One additional and important proof for the Catholic Church's claim to be the Church Christ established is, as we saw earlier, its unique ability to demonstrate continual existence from the time of Christ to the present day. This perpetuity was promised by the Lord in the final line of this marvelous passage:

And Jesus came and said to them, "All authority in heaven and on earth has been given to me. Go therefore and make disciples of all nations, baptizing them in the name of the Father and of the Son and of the Holy Spirit, teaching them to observe all that I have commanded you; and lo, I am with you always, to the close of the age." (Matt. 28:18-20)[73]

Summary

All of this evidence taken together shows that Jesus Christ established a particular Church, not some loose confederation of like-minded believers, or "denominations," within Christianity, as many people imagine He did. When He told Simon Peter, the first pope: "You are Peter, and on this rock *I will build my church*,[74] and the powers of death shall not prevail against it"[75] (Matt. 16:18),[76] he made a promise to His Church that He has faithfully kept since that very day.

SALVATION?

16. If you died tonight, would you go to heaven, and if so, why?

The answer to the first part of your question would depend on the condition of my soul when I die (and for the record, I hope I don't die for a long time, much less tonight).

If I'm in the state of grace when I die, I will go to heaven, guaranteed. But if I die in the state of mortal (i.e., deadly) sin[77] — willful and unrepentant rebellion against God — I will go to hell, also guaranteed.[78] As you can guess, I very much want to be in the state of grace when my time comes!

As for second part of your question — *why* would I go to heaven? — the only reason I would go to heaven would be because I died in the state of grace. And this grace is something God does for me, not something I do for Him. St. Paul makes this clear:

> God, who is rich in mercy, out of the great love with which he loved us, even when we were dead through our trespasses, made us alive together with Christ (by grace you have been saved), and raised us up with him, and made us sit with him in the heavenly places in Christ Jesus, that in the coming ages he might show the immeasurable riches of his grace in kindness toward us in Christ Jesus. *For by grace you have been saved through faith; and this is not your own doing, it is the gift of God, not because of works, lest any man should boast.* For we are his workmanship, created in Christ Jesus for good works, which God prepared beforehand, that we should walk in them. (Eph. 2:4-10)

We see how this transformation from sin to grace is likened to being raised from the dead. We once were dead in our sins, but now we are alive in Christ through grace. And the reverse process is, unfortunately, also possible. One who is alive in Christ can throw away that gift and kill his soul through mortal sin.

Note in particular the last part of the passage. God's grace is a *gift* to me. I can't boast about it because I didn't earn it. I am a sinner, in need of His grace. And He extends that grace to me, but I am always free to accept or reject it; free to remain in it or to throw it away and turn my back on it. If I accept His grace, embrace it, and live according to it, I will be saved. If I willfully reject His grace, I will go to the hot place, not because God sends me there, but because I chose it myself by my refusal. St. Paul spoke about being in the state of grace when he said,

> Note then the kindness and the severity of God: severity toward those who have fallen, but God's kindness to you, *provided you continue in his kindness*; otherwise you too will be cut off. (Rom. 11:22)

This section of Romans deals with the rejection of Christ by some Jews who lived at the time of His public ministry and their subsequent loss of salvation, which St. Paul likens to branches on a cultivated olive tree (i.e., the people of Israel, God's Chosen People) that were snapped off. The Christians He was addressing in Romans were predominately Gentiles whom He describes as branches from a wild olive tree that were "grafted on" to the cultivated tree, signifying their salvation.

This means that those who receive the gift of salvation by grace through faith (the Roman Christians to whom St. Paul was writing being a good example of this), are "in the state of grace." But, of course, they can choose to forfeit that gift of grace and lose their salvation,[79] a catastrophe that St. Paul warns Christians about repeatedly.

> The saying is sure: If we have died with him, we shall also live with him; if we endure, we shall

also reign with him; if we deny him, he also will deny us;[80] if we are faithless, he remains faithful — for he cannot deny himself. (2 Tim. 2:11-13)

Notice that St. Paul says "*if*" several times. This means there is a real possibility that the conditions for "living" and "reigning" with Christ in the life to come (i.e., salvation) might not be present in this life, namely "dying with Him" and "enduring." Worse yet, if you proactively *deny* the Lord, and die unrepentant in that condition, you'll face the hideous prospect of Him denying *you*. Consider this sobering reminder from Christ himself:

"So every one who acknowledges me before men, I also will acknowledge before my Father who is in heaven; *but whoever denies me before men, I also will deny before my Father who is in heaven.*" (Matt. 10:32-33)

St. John adds:

By this it may be seen who are the children of God, and who are the children of the devil: whoever does not do right is not of God, nor he who does not love his brother. For *this is the message which you have heard from the beginning, that we should love one another,*[81] and not be like Cain who was of the evil one and murdered his brother. And why did he murder him? Because his own deeds were evil and his brother's righteous. (1 John 3: 10-12)

Anyone who tells you that the central message of the Gospel is "justification by faith alone" doesn't understand the central message of the Gospel. St. John here reminds us, as does St. James in James 2, that faith in Christ, by itself, accomplishes nothing if it is not imbued with and completed by a grace-filled obedience to the Lord's command that we love one another, not through lip service, but through our concrete actions. Consider also what Christ said about those who will be saved and those who won't be:

> *"Why do you call me 'Lord, Lord,' and not do what I tell you?* Every one who comes to me and hears my words *and does them,* I will show you what he is like: he is like a man building a house, who dug deep, and laid the foundation upon rock; and when a flood arose, the stream broke against that house, and could not shake it, because it had been well built. But he who hears and does not *do* them is like a man who built a house on the ground without a foundation; against which the stream broke, and immediately it fell, and the ruin of that house was great." (Luke 6:46-49)

And what is it that Christ commands us to do? He answers this way:

> "This is my commandment, that you love one another as I have loved you. . . .You are my friends if you do what I command you." (John 15:12, 14)[82]

The practical reality of this commandment to love one another is that we are called to do "good works" (cf. Matt. 25:31-45; Luke 10:25-37; Rom. 2:5-8; Phil. 2:13; Col. 1:29; Rev. 20:12).

You can see how strongly Christ emphasizes the necessity of remaining in the state of grace:

> "As the Father has loved me, so have I loved you; abide in my love. If you keep my commandments, you will abide in my love, just as I have kept my Father's commandments and abide in his love." (John 15:9-10)

The phrase "remain in the state of grace" is simply another way of saying "Abide in my love." The meaning is the same.

This teaching is reinforced by St. James, who reminds us:

> What does it profit, my brethren, if a man says he has faith but has not works? Can his faith save him? If a brother or sister is ill-clad and in lack of daily food, and one of you says to them, "Go in peace, be warmed and filled," without giving them the things needed for the body, what does it profit? So faith by itself, if it has no works, is dead. . . .You see that a man is justified by works and not by faith alone. . . . For as the body apart from the spirit is dead, so faith apart from works is dead. (James 2: 14-17, 24, 26)

Notice that in the earlier passage Christ says that those who "come to me" (i.e., who have faith in Him[83]) must do more than merely hear His words if they want to be saved. They must do them. It's not enough simply to acknowledge Christ as Lord. This is very important, yes, but not sufficient. We must live out that faith in Him by doing those things He commands us to do[84] and by avoiding those things He commands us not to do.[85] As St. Paul warned, when the Judgment comes, God will inflict "vengeance upon those who do not know God and upon those who do not *obey* the gospel of our Lord Jesus" (2 Thes. 1:8).

According to Christ, St. Paul, and indeed all of the New Testament epistles and Gospels, this "obedience of faith"[86] is central to the life of a Christian who hopes to be saved, and it's another way of saying that we must live in the state of grace, which means obeying Christ's commands, avoiding sin, and clinging to Christ's grace for our salvation.

As St. Paul says in Ephesians 2:8-9, we are saved not by our own works, but by God's grace, which we appropriate through faith. And this grace is a gift from God, not something you and I can boast about. But never forget that the nature of this gift is that it enables us to now do something that would be impossible prior to our receiving it. Namely, God's gift of grace enables us to have saving faith in Christ, which is itself a gift. But this doesn't mean that God has faith in himself for us — we have to exercise that faith for ourselves. It's His gift, but it's a gift He wants us to use. And that gift of faith enables us to be obedient to His commands (i.e., good works). For, as St. Paul adds: "For we are his workmanship, created in Christ Jesus for good works, which God prepared beforehand, that we should walk in them" (Eph. 2:10). Faith and works go hand in hand, as St. John emphasizes in 1 John 3:23 (cf. Jas 2:1-26).

Finally, as we conclude the answer to this question about how and why one goes to heaven, think about being in the state of grace in light of this teaching from St. John the Apostle:

> By this we shall know that we are of the truth, and reassure our hearts before him whenever our hearts condemn us; for God is greater than our hearts, and he knows everything. Beloved, if our hearts do not condemn us, we have confidence before God; and we receive from him whatever we ask, because we keep his commandments and do what pleases him. And this is his commandment, that we should believe in the name of his Son Jesus Christ and love one another, just as he has commanded us. All who keep his commandments abide in him, and he in them. And by this we know that he abides in us, by the Spirit which he has given us. (1 John 3: 19-24; cf. 5:3)

Keep in mind that the converse of that statement is equally true: Anyone who refuses to keep His commandments will not abide in Christ. This is what Catholics mean by "falling into mortal sin." (cf. *Catechism of the Catholic Church*, 1033, 1037).

17. Why does the Catholic Church teach that by doing good works one can earn acceptance before God? This "works righteousness" approach to salvation is completely unbiblical and nullifies the grace of God (Rom. 11:6).

Contrary to what you've been told, this allegation is simply not true. It's both a misunderstanding of what the Catholic Church actually teaches and a misunderstanding of what the Bible says about what is required for salvation.

Let's begin by clearing up the first problem underlying your question. The Catholic Church does not now teach, nor has it ever taught, a doctrine of salvation based on "works righteousness." This is a common caricature raised by some non-Catholics, especially Fundamentalists and Evangelical Protestants. In fact, the notion of someone earning salvation is a heresy the Catholic Church has repeatedly condemned.[87] Rather, the Catholic Church has always upheld the apostolic teaching that we are, as St. Paul emphasized in Ephesians 2:8, saved "by grace through faith. . . . not because of works, lest anyone should boast . . ." We are told in this passage that the grace that saves us is a "gift of God," so we look to God, not ourselves, as the author and perfector of our salvation. But the Lord doesn't desire that we remain passive and inert in this process of our justification, sanctification, and eventual salvation.[88] He makes us His cooperators in this process. As St. Paul said in Ephesians 2, even our faith itself is a gift from God. Clearly, our faith is the instrument by which we receive and maintain the grace of our salvation, but notice what this entails: Our faith in Christ is a gift, but yet it is we who must exercise that faith in order for it to be efficacious. Or, to say it differently, God does not have faith in himself for us. We are the ones who have been enabled by His grace to have faith in Him — it is something we do. And it is, in a very real sense, a "work."

This, of course, is an issue that is hotly disputed by many within Protestantism, some agreeing with what I have just described, and others vehemently rejecting it. But the text of Scripture, here and elsewhere, is clear: God's grace is free to us, but we are called and enabled by Him to make use of that grace, not in some sort of crass bartering with God — "I do this, you do that" — but rather as His adopted sons and daughters who are now able to live out our faith by doing what Christ commands us.

The fact is, the Church proclaims exactly what Christ and the apostles proclaimed : namely, that we are all called to have faith in Christ and to be obedient to His commands. Being obedient to Christ's commands ("Why do you call me, 'Lord, Lord,' but do not do what I tell you?" [Luke 6:46]) is just as important as coming to Christ and believing in Him. In fact, as we saw above, Christ shows the futility of the man who claims that Christ is His Lord and Savior but who fails to act on that belief. It's the true believer, the authentic disciple of Christ who "comes to me and hears my words and does them" (Luke 6:47).

Consider also this often-overlooked reminder from the Lord:

> "As the Father has loved me, so have I loved you; abide in my love. If you keep my command-ments, you will abide in my love, just as I have kept my Father's commandments and abide in his love." (John 15:9-10)

This passage finds its echo in the Catholic teaching that in order to go to heaven, you must die in the state of grace. And notice that the Lord stipulates that you will abide in His love *if* you keep His commandments. The reverse is equally true: If you refuse to keep His com-mandments, you will not abide in His love. And if you don't abide in His love — and die unrepentant in that tragic state — you won't be saved. It's that simple.[89]

Salvation is a free gift of God for all, though only some will choose to embrace that gift of grace, repent and live out their faith through obedience to Christ (cf. Rom. 6:23; Titus 2:13-14; Eph. 2:8-9), not by their own useless "righteous" deeds (Titus 3:5; Heb. 6:1), but out of love for Christ, animated by His grace. "I can do all things through him who strengthens me" (Phil 4:13). And as St. John said, "Little children, let no one deceive you. He who *does right is righteous*, as he is righteous. He who commits sin is of the devil" (1 John 3:7-8).[90]

18. The Catholic Church's attempts to use James 2 to disprove *sola fide* (justification by faith alone) are just plain wrong. In James 2, the reference to Abraham being justified refers to his being justified before men, not before God. Verse 18 makes this clear. Which means that when James says in verse 24, "Ye see then how that by works a man is justified, and not by faith only" (King James Version), he is *not* referring to saving justification before God.

Wrong. The context of James 2 indeed refers to justification[91] before God, and not just before other humans. Look at the verse you mentioned: "But some one will say, 'You have faith and I have works.' Show me your faith apart from your works, and I by my works will show you my faith" (James 2:18). St. James is explaining the relationship between faith and works. Both are necessary for saving justification, but in different ways and for different reasons. St. Augustine put it this way:

> The preparation of man for the reception of grace is already a work of grace. This latter is needed to arouse and sustain our collaboration in justification through faith, and in sanctification through charity. God brings to completion in us what he has begun, "since he who completes

his work by cooperating with our will began by working so that we might will it."[92]

He also said:

Indeed we also work, but we are only collaborating with God who works, for his mercy has gone before us. It has gone before us so that we may be healed, and follows us so that once healed, we may be given life; it goes before us so that we may be called, and follows us so that we may be glorified; it goes before us so that we may live devoutly, and follows us so that we may always live with God: for without him we can do nothing.[93]

Saving faith is absolutely necessary[94] and is the starting point of our relationship with God. It is the means by which we appropriate our justification and live in righteousness before God.[95] As Ephesians 2:8-9 says, it's a gift of God, and it enables us, by God's grace, to repent of our sins and live out that faith through obedience[96] to the teachings of Christ.[97]

James, chapter 2, deals with the fact that faith alone is insufficient for salvation if it is divorced from a life of "good works," a term that bothers many Fundamentalists and Evangelical Protestants who have been taught that "works" are, per se, contrary to the gospel of grace. For them, St. James's statement, "You see that a man is justified by works and *not* by faith alone" is extremely problematic. It directly contradicts the Reformation notion of *sola fide* (justification by faith alone). This, by the way, is the main reason why Martin Luther wanted very much to eliminate the Epistle of James from the canon of the New Testament. He called it "an epistle of straw," saying he wanted to "throw Jimmy into the fire." He simply couldn't square his theory of justification by faith alone with St. James's clear teaching that we are *not* justified by faith alone.

As for your claim that this passage refers to being justified before men only, and not before God (which is the very heart of the issue for saving justification), a close examination of James 2 reveals that his mention of Abraham's intention to sacrifice his son Isaac was not something done as a sign to others. In fact, if you read carefully the account of Abraham's righteous deed in Genesis 22:1-12, you'll see that when God gave him the command to take Isaac up the mountain and sacrifice him, no one else was there to hear God say this. It was private, between God and Abraham only. Even Isaac did not know what was to happen.

Second, there was no one else present when Abraham attempted to sacrifice Isaac and was stopped at the last moment by the angel. In Genesis 22:5, Abraham stopped at the base of the mountain, or at some distance further away, and instructed his servants to stay behind and tend the donkey while he and Isaac continued on to the summit.

Third, there is every reason to believe that, far from performing this deed in front of others, Abraham told no one, not even Isaac, about what God had told him to do. If he had spread the word that he was about to sacrifice his only son, his neighbors might have locked him up in the loony bin (or worse!). After all, he was already quite an old man when God miraculously gave him and his previously barren wife, Sarah, a child in their old age.[98] Just imagine how his friends and family would have reacted in horror and disbelief if Abraham had let anyone else know what God had commanded him to do. Without a doubt, there was no audience of fellow human beings whom Abraham was trying to impress or be justified to. Rather, this was between him and God alone.

So, think carefully about what St. James says: "Was not Abraham our father justified by works, when he offered his son Isaac upon the altar? You see that faith was active along with his works, and faith was completed by works, and the Scripture was fulfilled which says, 'Abraham believed God, and it was reckoned to him as righteousness'; and he was called the friend of God" (James 2:21-23). It's clear from the context that *both* his faith and his obedience to God's commands (good works) were "credited to him as righteousness." And this is exactly what the Catholic Church teaches (and which, sadly, virtually all of Protestantism rejects). God's comment in Genesis 22:12 makes it clear that Abraham's faith and works were not being presented before others, but before God himself: "Now I know that you fear God, seeing you have not withheld your son, your only son, from me" (Gen. 22:12).

So you see, justification involves both faith and obedience. Both are necessary, as St. John explained:

> Beloved, if our hearts do not condemn us, we have confidence before God; and we receive from him whatever we ask, *because we keep his commandments and do what pleases him.* And this is his commandment, that we should believe in the name of his Son Jesus Christ [i.e., "faith"] and love one another, just as he has commanded us [i.e., "good works"]. All who keep his commandments abide in him, and he in them. And by this we know that he abides in us, by the Spirit which he has given us. (1 John 3:21-24)

19. The Bible is clear that born-again believers cannot lose their salvation: "I write this to you who believe in the name of the Son of God, that you may know that you have eternal life" (1 John 5:13; cf. Rom. 8:28-29). John 10:27-29 says, "My sheep hear my voice, and I know them, and they follow me; and I give them eternal life, and they shall never perish, and no one shall snatch them out of myy hand. My Father, who has given them to me, is greater than all, and no one is able to snatch them out of the Father's hand." Why does the Catholic Church teach the opposite: that Christians can lose their salvation? In any dispute between the Catholic Church and the Word of God, I'll stick with the Word of God.

I heartily agree with you that one should always follow God's Word, but you're incorrect in thinking there's a "dispute" between what the Bible says and what the Catholic Church teaches on this issue. The fact is, the Bible is clear that Christians can lose their salvation. Consider these passages that demonstrate this:

> Now I am speaking to you Gentiles. Inasmuch then as I am an apostle to the Gentiles, I magnify my ministry in order to make my fellow Jews jealous, and thus save some of them. For if their rejection means the reconciliation of the world, what will their acceptance mean but life from the dead? If the dough offered as first fruits is holy, so is the whole lump; and if the root is holy, so are the branches. But if some of the branches were broken off, and you, a wild olive shoot, were grafted in their place to share the richness of the olive tree, do not boast over the branches. If you do boast, remember it is not you that support the root, but the root that supports you. You will say, "Branches were broken off so that I might be grafted in." That is true. They were broken off because of their unbelief, but you stand fast only through faith. So do not become proud, but stand in awe. For if God did not spare the natural branches, neither will he spare you. Note then the kindness and the severity of God: severity toward those who have

fallen, but God's kindness to you, provided you continue in his kindness; otherwise you too will be cut off. (Rom. 11:13-22)

This saying is sure: If we have died with him, we shall also live with him; if we endure, we shall also reign with him; if we deny him, he also will deny us; if we are faithless, he remains faithful, for he cannot deny himself.[99] (2 Tim. 2:11-13)

Therefore, brethren, since we have confidence to enter the sanctuary by the blood of Jesus, by the new and living way which he opened for us through the curtain, that is, through his flesh, and since we have a great priest over the house of God, let us draw near with a true heart in full assurance of faith, with our hearts sprinkled clean from an evil conscience and our bodies washed with pure water. Let us hold fast the confession of our hope without wavering, for he who promised is faithful; and let us consider how to stir up one another to love and good works, not neglecting to meet together, as is the habit of some, but encouraging one another, and all the more as you see the Day drawing near. For if we sin deliberately after receiving the knowledge of the truth, there no longer remains a sacrifice for sins, but a fearful prospect of judgment, and a fury of fire which will consume the adversaries. A man who has violated the law of Moses dies without mercy at the testimony of two or three witnesses. How much worse punishment do you think will be deserved by the man who has spurned the Son of God, and profaned the blood of the covenant by which he was sanctified, and outraged the Spirit of grace? (Heb. 10:19-29)

For if, after they have escaped the defilements of the world through the knowledge of our Lord and Savior Jesus Christ, they are again entangled in them and overpowered, the last state has become worse for them than the first. For it would have been better for them never to have known the way of righteousness than after knowing it to turn back from the holy commandment delivered to them. It has happened to them according to the true proverb, The dog turns back to his own vomit, and the sow is washed only to wallow in the mire. (2 Peter 2:20-22)

And let's not forget the Lord's words in the Gospels. In the Parable of the Unforgiving Servant, he makes it very clear that one can gain salvation and then forfeit it through wicked actions (cf. Matt. 18:21-35). In this passage, we see the perfect parallel for the biblical teaching on salvation: The servant who owes a huge sum of money is analogous to the guilty sinner — you and me. He pleads for mercy to the master he owes the money to (who is analogous to God), and having pity on the man, the master cancels his entire debt and sends him on his way, his financial burden lifted from his shoulders (analogous to God's forgiving our sins when we repent). However, because the first man acted wickedly toward the second man, who only owed him a very small sum, the master reinstated the entire debt! This chilling element is analogous to what happens when a Christian (yes, a Bible-believing, born-again Christian) refuses to live according to Christ's law to "love one another" (John 13:34).[100]

The Lord's final comment here makes the point perfectly clear that one can lose his salvation: "So also my heavenly Father will do to every one of you, if you do not forgive your brother from your heart." (verse 35).[101] In other words, God will punish us for our bad works (sins) and reward us for our good works (obedience).[102] Although there's nothing we can do to earn salvation,[103] the Bible is clear that our faith-filled acts of obedience to Christ are meritorious and pleasing in God's eyes and He will reward us for them with eternal life.[104]

To conclude, let's consider a question that's popular among Fundamentalists and Evangelical Protestants: "Have you been saved?" To them, salvation is a one-time event. You repent, accept Jesus Christ as your personal Lord and Savior, say the sinner's prayer (or some variant), and you are "saved." In their view, it's a done deal, and no matter what might happen in the person's life from that point forward, he has been "saved" and is absolutely assured of going to heaven when he dies. But as we've seen above, the Bible simply does not teach that notion of being "once saved, always saved." If someone turns to a life of unrepentant sin after once being saved by grace, he can lose his salvation. If he dies in this state, he will go to hell. As St. Paul said, "The wages of sin is death" (Rom. 6:23).[105]

All Christians have what is called a moral assurance of salvation, though not an absolute one. This means that we can always trust that Christ will never go back on His word, His promise of eternal life to those who love Him. We ourselves are quite capable, if we throw away His love and turn away from Him, to ruin our opportunity for salvation.[106]

In response to the question, "Have you been saved?" Catholics and all other Christians should respond with biblical truth, saying, I have been redeemed and saved by God's grace through faith (cf. Eph. 2:8), I am being saved and am working out my salvation with fear and trembling (cf. Phil. 2:13; 1 Peter 1:8-9), my salvation is nearer now than it was yesterday (cf. Rom. 13:11), and trusting solely in God's grace, I pray that I will be saved (cf. 1 Cor. 3:15) by remaining in the state of grace and friendship with Him until the end of my life (cf. Matt. 24:13; Rom. 11:22).

THE PAPACY

20. What makes you think Peter had any special authority or primacy among the apostles? The Bible nowhere says anything about Peter being the first

pope! The Catholic Church added the doctrine of the papacy to God's Word.

Perhaps you aren't as familiar with the biblical evidence as you think you are. One telling point about Simon Peter is that among the Twelve Apostles, he is mentioned by name some one hundred ninety-five times in the pages of the New Testament. The next most often mentioned apostle is St. John, who is mentioned by name twenty-nine times. After St. John, the other apostles appear by name far less often. So you can see a striking prominence for Simon Peter, simply on the basis of how often he is mentioned by name.

Also, there are an overwhelming number of scriptural episodes that point to a special primacy among the apostles that St. Peter had. For one thing, whenever the apostles are all listed by name as a group,[107] he is always first, and Judas, the Lord's betrayer, is always last. More interestingly, usually the apostles aren't mentioned by name as a group. Instead, we see phrases such as "Peter and the others,"[108] which indicate that it was understood that Simon Peter represented the college of apostles.

Only Simon, among all the other personages of the New Testament, received a name change (cf. Matt. 16:18-19). This signified his status as the "rock" upon which Christ would build His Church. He was also chosen by Christ to be the one who would receive "the keys of the kingdom of heaven." He was told that whatever he personally bound on earth would be bound in heaven and what he loosed on earth would be loosed in heaven. And though the rest of the apostles received this authority in a general way in Matthew 18:18, it was to Simon Peter alone that Christ conferred this power in Matthew 16:18-19.

It was to Peter that Christ called to come out of the boat and walk on water (Matt. 14:25-33). It was from Simon Peter's fishing boat that Christ preached to the crowds that pressed against him on the shore of the Lake of Galilee (cf. Luke 5:3). St. John deferred to Peter at the tomb, even though he was younger and ran there faster than Peter, waiting for Peter to enter ahead of him (John 20:6). It was to Simon Peter, first among all the apostles, that Christ's resurrection was revealed and the first among the apostles to whom Christ appeared after His resurrection (Mark 16:7).

In Luke 22:31-32 we see the Lord confer upon Peter a special role among the apostles: "Simon, Simon, behold, Satan demanded to have you, that he might sift you like wheat, but I have prayed for you that your faith may not fail; and when you have turned again, strengthen your brethren." Not that he speaks first in the plural form ("Satan demands to have you" [plural]) but in the second passage, he speaks in the singular form to Simon Peter alone: "But I have prayed for you (singular) that your (singular) faith may not fail."[109] Similarly, in Luke 22: 31-32, Christ tells Peter three times to "feed my sheep," an indication of his special role as the pastor of the flock.

Peter leads the other apostles in choosing a replacement for Judas, who had committed suicide (Acts 1:13-26). He preaches the first post-Pentecost sermon, leading some three thousand people into the Church through baptism. The first miracle performed after Pentecost was by Peter (Acts 3:1-10), and it was he who led the apostles and faced down the Sanhedrin in Acts 4: 1-12.

In Acts 10:9-16, God delivers revelation to Peter that Gentiles could now enter the Church without the need to observe Jewish Kosher food laws, and this teaching Peter made binding on the whole Church at the Council of Jerusalem in Acts 15. Repeatedly in the pages of the New Testament, Peter is shown to have had a unique primacy and authority among the Twelve Apostles. And as a final example of that fact, remember that the great St. Paul himself, after his conversion to Christ and time spent in prayer and preparation, did not begin his own public ministry until he had first gone up to Jerusalem and checked in with Peter (cf. Gal. 1:18). If nothing else, that alone should give you pause and make you reconsider your argument that Peter had no special primacy.[110]

21. I am Greek Orthodox. You Catholics have deviated from the true faith and tradition of the apostles by claiming that the bishop of Old Rome, the "pope,"

has authority over other bishops. That's a medieval Roman invention and was not what the Fathers of the early Church taught or believed.

This is a common argument raised by Orthodox Christians, but it's completely incorrect. The evidence from the early Church is vast and compelling, that shows that the bishop of Rome did indeed have a unique authority.

Perhaps the greatest of the Eastern early Church Fathers was St. John Chrysostom, the patriarch of Constantinople.[111] The Eucharistic Liturgy he composed and codified can serve as an example that the early Church did indeed regard the bishop of Rome as having authority over other bishops. Rather than belabor the point with a mountain of similar quotes from other early Church Fathers showing that the early Church indeed recognized the bishop of Rome as having a unique authority,[112] let it suffice to read what this great Eastern patriarch wrote on the subject of the authority of Simon Peter and, by extension, his successors, the popes:

> Seest thou how He [Christ], His own self, leads Peter on to high thoughts of Him, and reveals Himself, and implies that He is Son of God by these two promises? For those things which are peculiar to God alone, (both to absolve sins, and to make the church incapable of overthrow

in such assailing waves, and to exhibit a man that is a fisher more solid than any rock, while all the world is at war with him), these He promises Himself to give; as the Father, speaking to Jeremiah, said, He would make him as "a brazen pillar, and as a wall"; him to one nation only, this man in every part of the world.

I would fain inquire then of those who desire to lessen the dignity of the Son, which manner of gifts were greater, those which the Father gave to Peter, or those which the Son gave him? *For the Father gave to Peter the revelation of the Son; but the Son gave him to sow that of the Father and that of Himself in every part of the world; and to a mortal man He entrusted the authority over all things in heaven, giving him the keys; who extended the church to every part of the world, and declared it to be stronger than heaven.* "For heaven and earth shall pass away, but my word shall not pass away." How then is He less, who hath given such gifts, hath effected such things? And these things I say, not dividing the works of Father and Son ("for all things are made by Him, and without Him was nothing made which was made"): but bridling the shameless tongue of them that dare so to speak. But see, throughout all, His authority: "I say unto thee, Thou art Peter; I will build the Church; I will give thee the keys of heaven."[113]

22. Pope Gregory the Great rejected the title of "Universal Bishop." That's exactly what we Orthodox are saying to you Catholics: The Pope is wrong to claim that he is the head of the whole Church. He is not, as Pope Gregory himself asserted. He is first among equals and nothing more. Why don't you follow what Pope Gregory said?

It seems that you are unaware of the details of this story. The facts of the matter demonstrate just the opposite of your claim here. Specifically, as we'll see in a moment, Pope Gregory the Great[114] did condemn the use of the term "Universal Bishop," but he did not in any way repudiate the two thousand-year old Catholic teaching regarding the primacy of the bishop of Rome.

But first, before we examine the evidence, it's interesting and instructive to note that it was an Eastern bishop, John the Faster, the patriarch of Constantinople,[115] who caused this ruckus in the first place, because it was he who claimed for himself the title of "Ecumenical Patriarch (also referred to as "Universal Bishop")[116] — an Eastern innovation that needed to be corrected more than once by the pope in Rome.

Catholic historian Father Adrian Fortescue commented trenchantly on this matter: "Opposed to it Gregory assumed the title borne ever since by his successors. 'He refuted the name "universal" and first of all began to write himself "servant of the servants of God" at the beginning of his letters, with sufficient humility, leaving to all his successors this hereditary evidence of his meekness' (Johannes Diaconus, Vita S. Gregorii, II, i, in P. L., LXV, 87). Nevertheless the patriarchs of Constantinople kept their 'Ecumenical' title till it became part of their official style. The Orthodox patriarch subscribes himself still 'Archbishop of Constantinople, New Rome, and Ecumenical Patriarch.' But it is noticeable that even Photius (d. 891) never dared use the word when writing to Rome. The Catholic Church has never admitted it [i.e., permitted its usage]. It became a symbol of Byzantine arrogance and the Byzantine schism. In 1024 the Emperor St. Basil II (963-1025) tried to persuade Pope John XIX (1024-1033) to acknowledge it. The pope seems to have been ready to do so, but an outburst of indignation throughout the West and a stern letter from Abbot William of Dijon made him think better of it."[117]

While John the Faster was the first Eastern bishop to attempt this, he was not the last. Five centuries later, for example, in 1053, Michael Caerularius, the patriarch of Constantinople,[118] again tried to arrogate this title for himself, and Pope Leo IX chastised him for it, saying: "How lamentable and detestable is the sacrilegious usurpation by which you everywhere boast yourself to be the Universal Patriarch."[119]

We must be careful here to understand the nature of this argument, which is often employed by Orthodox Christians and some Protestants. In their view (keeping in mind here that most Orthodox seem to be unaware that the "Universal Bishop" problem was really an Eastern aberration, not a Roman one), the fact that Pope Gregory the Great denounced that title is some sort of proof that the pope himself cannot therefore claim to have jurisdiction of primacy over other bishops. So let's analyze this objection and see if it has merit.

Keep in mind that Pope Gregory understood the term "Universal Bishop" to have been used in a particular way, one that he believed was incompatible with the office of the patriarch of Constantinople. As I wrote elsewhere, "Two things can be meant by this phrase. 'Universal Bishop' can mean either a bishop over the entire Church (universal jurisdiction), while not denying the individual authority of local bishops, or it can imply that the bishop who claims this title sees himself as a bishop of all other bishops — kind of a 'super bishop' to whom all other bishops should look to as their bishop. This would imply that the other bishops of the world were not truly bishops in the fullest sense, and that there was a single bishop for the entire world.

"When Gregory attacked the title 'Universal Bishop,' the evidence shows that he was condemning the latter definition, not the former. This is clear from his words in *Epistle 68*: 'For if one, as (John the Faster) supposes, is Universal Bishop, it remains that you are not bishops.' Gregory was it not objecting to the term 'Universal Bishop' as if it meant that the pope didn't have universal primacy among the college of bishops. Rather, he was reproaching (what he viewed as) the arrogance displayed by the then-patriarch of Constantinople.

"In his actions and writings, is was very clear that he (like bishops everywhere, East and West) recognized that the Apostolic See in Rome had a certain jurisdictional authority over other dioceses, including Constantinople and the other patriarchates. Contrary to what some Orthodox and Protestant polemicists would have you believe, the evidence shows that throughout his entire pontificate, Pope Gregory neither denied nor appeared to deny papal authority and primacy. This is evident from his many epistles, in which he admonished, instructed, directed, rebuked, encouraged, and generally guided with a firm but friendly hand the various churches around the world."[120] Consider these facts:[121]

In *Epistle 10*, Pope Gregory set forth the necessary qualities for suitable candidates for bishop. He asked his brother bishops throughout the Church to follow those guidelines in their decisions regarding new bishops. In the same epistle, he rejected some candidates for bishop who had already been approved by other bishops. These elements make it clear that Pope Gregory recognized his own authority to determine general ecclesiastical policy on who could and could not be ordained a bishop, as did his brothers in the episcopate.

In *Epistle 17*, we see Pope Gregory intervening in the affairs of the church at Firmum. He canceled a debt owed to that church by a layman. If he had no jurisdiction over that church, or if other bishops did not acknowledge and submit to papal authority, the Pope could not have cancelled the debt of someone who lived within the boundaries of that other church. What's more, his decision was adhered to by the church at Firmum. If the notion of the pope — the bishop of Rome — having a special authority that extended the borders of his own diocese was truly alien to the early Church, as our Orthodox and Protestant friends commonly, though erroneously, assert, you can be certain that Firmum and other churches would have complained that Pope Gregory had overstepped his authority by meddling in their affairs. But that did not happen.

In *Epistle 81*, Pope Gregory restored Bishop Maximus to communion with the Catholic Church. Pope Gregory had the power to excommunicate other bishops, as well as to restore them. Bishop Maximus approached the Pope repentantly, which shows that he, too, recognized the primacy and jurisdiction of the Roman See.

Pope Gregory also wrote: "And although our most pious Emperor allows nothing unlawful to be done there, yet, lest perverse men, taking occasion of your assembly, should seek opportunity of cajoling you in favoring this name of superstition, or should think of holding a synod about some other matter, with the view of introducing it therein by cunning contrivances — though without the authority and consent of the Apostolic See nothing that might be passed would have any force, nevertheless, before Almighty God I conjure and warn you, that the assent of none of you be obtained by any blandishments, any bribes, any threats whatever; but, having regard to the eternal judgment, acquit ye yourselves salubriously and unanimously in opposition to wrongful aims; and, supported by pastoral constancy and apostolical authority, keep out the robber and the wolf that would rush in, and give no way to him that rages for the tearing of the Church asunder; nor allow, through any cajolery, a synod to be held on this subject, which indeed would not be a legitimate one, nor to be called a synod. . . . For if any one, as we do not believe will be the case, should disregard in any part this present writing, let him know that he is segregated from the peace of the blessed Peter, the Prince of the Apostles."[122]

In this letter, Pope Gregory unequivocally emphasizes the primacy and authority of the bishop of Rome which, he says, is an extension of the ministry of "Peter, the Prince of the Apostles." He obviously believed that no canon law had any validity unless it had been approved by the "authority and consent of the Apostolic See." And for him to make that claim is ample evidence that he understood his role as bishop of Rome to entail universal jurisdiction over the laws of the Church. His brother bishops around the world recognized and acknowledged this as well.

In *Epistle 59*, Gregory intervened into the affairs of another Church regarding the disciplining of another bishop:

[I]t is exceedingly doubtful whether he says such things to us sincerely, or in fact because he is being attacked by his fellow-bishops: for, as to his saying that he is subject to the Apostolic See,[123] if any fault is found in bishops, I know not what bishop is not subject to it.

But when no fault requires it to be otherwise, all according to the principle of humility are equal.[124] Nevertheless, do you speak with the aforesaid most eloquent Martin as seems good to your Fraternity. For it is for you to consider what should be done; and we have replied to you briefly on the case, because we ought not to believe indiscriminately men that are even unknown to us. If, however, you, who see him before you in person, are of opinion that anything more definite should be said to him, we commit this to your charity, being sure of your love in the grace of Almighty God. And what you do regard without doubt as having been done by us.

There are three important elements to take note of in this statement. First, Pope Gregory states that all other bishops, not just those in the West, are subject to the authority of the Apostolic See. Second, he delegates his authority to another bishop in the matter of the punishment of a third party, the accused bishop under discussion. And third, it's clear that

Pope Gregory holds a certain primacy of authority over other bishops because the accused bishop appealed to him in the first place, and the other bishops await his decision regarding punishment or correction.

Elsewhere, demonstrating his conviction that the bishop of Rome's decrees, even in non-doctrinal matters, were binding and immutable by other bishops, Pope Gregory wrote: "This he did as knowing such reverence to be paid by the faithful to the Apostolic See that what had been settled by its decree no molestation of unlawful usurpation would thereafter shake. . . . For, though what has once been sanctioned by the authority of the Apostolic See has no lack of validity, yet we do, over and above, once more corroborate by our authority in all respects all things that were ordained by our predecessor[125] for quiet in this matter."[126]

And if there is any doubt left that Pope Gregory the Great, while denouncing Patriarch John the Faster for arrogating to himself the title of "Universal Bishop," in no way expressed or implied by his words or his actions that the bishop of Rome did not have universal primacy, consider these pointed words written by Pope Gregory, almost as if to drive the last nail in the coffin of this spurious argument:

> For as to what they say about the Church of Constantinople, who can doubt that it is subject to the Apostolic See, as both the most pious lord the emperor and our brother the bishop of that

city continually acknowledge? Yet, if this or any other Church has anything that is good, I am prepared in what is good to imitate even my inferiors,[127] while prohibiting them from things unlawful.[128]

23. The pope is a sinner, like anyone else. How can you possibly believe in papal infallibility when it's clear that popes make mistakes (sometimes big ones)?

You're right, all the popes, including the first pope, St. Peter himself, have been sinners in need of God's grace and mercy. That has always been the Catholic Church's teaching. But that Catholic doctrine of papal infallibility has nothing whatsoever to do with the pope's sinfulness or sanctity. Your question is based on a common misunderstanding that infallibility (i.e., the inability to formally teach error) equals impeccability (i.e., the inability to commit sin).

Although the Church has been blessed with a long succession of saintly pontiffs over the last century and beyond, it's not difficult to find examples of scoundrels who have sat on the Chair of Peter. Notorious popes such as Alexander VI[129] were known for their debauchery. They gave public scandal in ways large and small, but history shows that the number of truly wicked popes has been mercifully quite small. Even so, the bad popes shocked their contemporaries (and even us today) with their fornication, adultery, lying, cheating, and even, at times, murder.[130] There is no use denying these facts, nor can they be defended or explained away. The depredations of that handful of "bad popes" are tragic chapters in the history of the Catholic Church, but even so, they don't disprove by one particle the Church's teaching on papal infallibility.

The doctrine of papal infallibility was expressed this way by Vatican Council I: "[F]aithfully adhering to the tradition received from the beginning of the Christian faith, to the glory of God our savior, for the exaltation of the Catholic religion and for the salvation of the Christian people, with the approval of the Sacred Council, we teach and define as a divinely revealed dogma that when the Roman Pontiff speaks *ex cathedra,* that is, when, in the exercise of his office as shepherd and teacher of all Christians, in virtue of his supreme apostolic authority, he defines a doctrine concerning faith or morals to be held by the whole Church, he possesses, by the divine assistance promised to him in blessed Peter, that infallibility which the divine Redeemer willed his Church to enjoy in defining doctrine concerning faith or morals. Therefore, such definitions of the Roman Pontiff are of themselves, and not by the consent of the Church, irreformable."[131]

As you can see, there's nothing here about the pope's personal conduct, good or bad. Papal infallibility is grounded on the principle of Christ being true to His promises to guide and protect His Church, in particular through the ministry of St. Peter and his successors, the bishops of Rome.[132] The Lord's promises, such as, "Whatever you bind on earth with be bound in heaven, and whatever you loose on earth will be loosed in heaven" (Matt. 16:18-19), and, "He who hears you hears me, and he who rejects you rejects me" (Luke 10:16), would be impossible to keep if He hadn't established some way to ensure that Peter and His successors did not lead the Church into error through teaching as true what was actually erroneous. The implication of these and other verses commonly brought forward as biblical evidence for the infallibility of the pope and the Church itself is that Christ guarantees the teaching of the pope to be free from error so that the Lord, in heaven, could bind and loose in heaven what was bound and loosed on earth, and so that when the pope teaches, Christ indeed is teaching through him (cf. Luke 10:16).

The sins any pope commits, whether great or small, do not negate the power of God's grace to protect him from teaching error.[133] All Protestants would agree with this, at least in principle, since they accept as inspired and authoritative the scriptural writings of other sinful men, such as King David (who had committed murder and adultery) and Simon Peter (who had abandoned the Lord and denied Him three times). One need not look any further for biblical evidence that God's grace is more powerful than man's sin and that

God can still use sinful men to teach infallibly. St. Paul expressed this truth so well when he wrote:

> [The Lord] said to me, "My grace is sufficient for you, for my power is made perfect in weakness." I will all the more gladly boast of my weaknesses, that the power of Christ may rest upon me.[134]

> Now to him who is able to do all things more abundantly than we desire or understand, according to the power that worketh in us.[135]

THE HOLY SPIRIT

24. The Holy Spirit does not proceed from the Father *and* the Son, as you Catholics erroneously say in your Creed. He proceeds from the Father alone (cf. John 15:26). Also, there is no mention in Scripture that He proceeds from the Son. That notion is a man-made addition, starting with St. Augustine.

For the sake of clarity, let's begin by stating the teaching of the Catholic Church on this issue: "The Holy Spirit proceeds from the Father and from the Son as from a single principle through a single spiration [*vis spirativa* (i.e., sending, or 'breathing' forth the Holy Spirit)]."

In Latin, the phrase "and the son" is *Filioque*. This one small term has been the focus of a vast conflagration of controversy between Catholics and Orthodox over the last one thousand years. It's impossible to attempt to condense the entire squabble into only a few brief pages, but let's at least consider the basic issues and look at what the Bible does, in fact, say about the procession of the Holy Spirit.

The background to this controversy can be summed up by saying that the Ecumenical Councils of Nicea (A.D. 325) and Constantinople (A.D. 381) formally taught the doctrine that the Holy Spirit proceeds from the Father. The creeds that arose out of these two councils contain this affirmation: "I believe in the Holy Spirit, the Lord, the Giver of Life, Who proceeds from the Father. With the Father and Son he is worshipped and glorified. . . . "This was the accepted formula in the East and the West for the next two centuries.

However, in the West, especially, the persistent heresy of Arianism, which vociferously argued that Christ was not the true God and that the Holy Spirit, likewise, was not a Divine Person, remained a severe problem even into the Middle Ages. Catholic theologians, Scripture scholars, and bishops whose task it was to refute the claims of the Arians developed an ever deeper insight into the theological ramifications of the truth that the Holy Spirit proceeds from the Father. They recognized, for the reasons we'll see as we continue, that the Holy Spirit also proceeds from the Son. This insight, which the Latin term *Filioque* expresses, became common in the Creed as it was recited in the West, and eventually was formally affirmed by the Council of Toledo in A.D. 589.

One reason why the Church affirmed this truth had to do with the fact that the Nicene Creed emphasizes that Christ, the Second Person of the Blessed Trinity, is the "only-begotten son of the Father." He is eternally generated by the Father. This eternal generation, however, is not true of the Holy Spirit. If the Spirit proceeded from the Father alone, and not also from the Son, what then would be the essential distinction between the Son being the "only-begotten of the Father,"[136] and the Holy Spirit proceeding from the Father alone?

A.J. Mass wrote: "As to the Sacred scripture, the inspired writers call the Holy Ghost the 'Spirit of his Son'" (Gal. 4:6), the 'Spirit of Christ (Rom. 8:9), the 'Spirit of Jesus Christ' (Phil. 1:19), just as they call Him the 'Spirit of your Father' (Matt. 10:20) and the 'Spirit of God' (1 Cor. 2:11). Hence they attribute to the Holy Ghost the same relation to the Son as to the Father." [137]

This statement is echoed by Catholic theologian Ludwig Ott, who wrote: "That the Holy Ghost proceeds from the Father and from the Son as from One Single Principle and through One Single spiration, is clear from John 16:15: 'All that the Father has is mine.' If the Son, by virtue of his eternal generation from the Father, possesses everything that the Father possesses except the Fatherhood and the unregeneratedness, which are not communicable, then He must also possess the power of spiration, and with it the being a principle in relation to the Holy Ghost."[138]

Now let's consider the biblical evidence that the Holy Spirit also proceeds from the Son, and not from the Father alone. Keep in mind that to "proceed" from the Father and the Son means that the Father and the Son "send" the Holy Spirit.[139] In the same way that the Father sends the Son[140] and He sends the Holy Spirit,[141] so, too, Jesus Christ, the Second Person of the Blessed Trinity, sends the Holy Spirit:

> "But when the Counselor [i.e., Holy Spirit] comes, whom I shall send to you from the Father, even the Spirit of truth, who proceeds from the Father, he will bear witness to me."[142] (John 15:26)

We see here a direct allusion to the Filioque, that the Spirit is sent by the Father *and* the Son. Christ says the Spirit "proceeds" from the Father and is also "sent" by the Son.

> "Nevertheless I tell you the truth: it is to your advantage that I go away, for if I do not go away, the Counselor will not come to you; but if I go, I will send him to you." (John 16:7)

> And when he had said this, he breathed on them, and said to them, "Receive the Holy Spirit. If you forgive the sins of any, they are forgiven; if you retain the sins of any, they are retained." (John 20:22)

Here the Son sends the Holy Spirit onto the apostles. Now look at these additional verses that show the same action: the Son sending the Spirit.

> Being therefore exalted at the right hand of God, and having received from the Father the promise of the Holy Spirit, he [Christ] has poured out this which you see and hear. (Acts 2:33)

> He [Christ] saved us, not because of deeds done by us in righteousness, but in virtue of his own mercy, by the washing of regeneration and renewal in the Holy Spirit, which he poured out upon us richly through Jesus Christ our Savior, so that we might be justified by his grace and become heirs in hope of eternal life. (Titus 3:5-7)

Christ's "pouring out" the Holy Spirit is the equivalent of the Holy Spirit proceeding from Him.

And a final tantalizing tidbit of evidence supporting historicity of this Catholic teaching comes from Catholic journalist John Allen, who wrote:

> Father Johannes Grohe, an Opus Dei priest who teaches church history at Santa Croce [Pontifical University in Rome], spoke on the history of Church councils. He offered several interesting nuggets, such as the fact that a regional council in Persia in [A.D.] 410 produced one of the earliest insertions of the famed Filioque clause into the Creed, specifying that the Holy Spirit proceeds

from the Father "and from the Son."[143] This council, as Grohe points out, was an Eastern affair, and its adoption of the Filioque came out of the rich theological reflection of early Persian Christianity. Hence the notion that the Filioque is solely an imposition of the medieval Western Church upon the East, born of later controversies between Rome and Byzantium, is historically dubious.[144]

SACRED TRADITION

25. Can you show me a single, extra-biblical Catholic "tradition" that is necessary for me as a Christian? If you can't, then you will have proven that Scripture is our sole, sufficient, rule of faith.

I can show you plenty of them, but the one that's most likely to get your attention is the canon of the New Testament.[145] That's part of God's revelation to the Church that comes down to us entirely outside of the Bible. There is no "inspired table of contents" anywhere in the Bible that will tell you which books belong in the Bible.

Think about it: You must rely on that Tradition to know what the New Testament itself is, and you do accept it, by virtue of the fact that you have a Bible. Without that Tradition of the canon, you simply can't know which books make up the New Testament.

And remember, too, that those epistles and Gospels are inspired by God himself[146] and were given to the Church through revelation. The Catholic Church gives all the glory to God for this. The Church did not make those books inspired; God did. Similarly, the Catholic Church did not make them "canonical"; God did, by the very fact that He revealed them. But it's no less true that the Catholic Church received this revelation from God and that the Church — which, don't forget, had been commissioned by Christ to authoritatively teach the meaning of the Inspired Scriptures[147] — was charged with the twofold task of both interpreting Scripture as well as organizing and perpetuating its existence. What this means is that the Catholic Church, which had been entrusted with the great gift of the New Testament canon, handed on that revelation faithfully and accurately.

To make the point about the canon, I wrote elsewhere that "*sola scriptura* becomes 'canon' fodder as soon as the Catholic asks the Protestant to explain how the books of the Bible got into the Bible. Under the *sola scriptura* rubric, Scripture exists in an absolute epistemological vacuum, since it and the veracity of its contents 'dependeth not upon the testimony of any man or church.'[148] If that's true, how then can anyone know with certitude what belongs in Scripture in the first place? The answer is you can't. Without recognizing the trustworthiness of the magisterium, endowed with Christ's own teaching authority,[149] and the living apostolic Tradition of the Church (1 Cor. 11:1; 2 Thes. 2:15; 2 Tim. 2:2), there is no way to know for certain which books belong in Scripture and which do not. As soon as Protestants begin to appeal to the canons drawn up by this or that Church Father, or this or that council, they immediately concede defeat, since they are forced to appeal to the very 'testimony of man and Church' that they claim to not need."[150]

STATUES, ICONS, AND THE SIN OF IDOLATRY

26. Why does the Catholic Church hide the Second Commandment, "You shall have no other gods before me"?

The Catholic Church does not "hide" any part of the commandments. Rather, the difference between how Catholics and Protestants number the commandments stems from the issue of how we interpret the prohibition on idolatry in Exodus 20:17 a nd Deuteronomy 5:6-8. Let's look at how the Catholic Church numbers the commandments:

I. Thus shalt have no strange gods before me.
II. Thus shalt not take the name of the Lord thy God in vain.
III. Keep holy the Sabbath.
IV. Honor your father and your mother.

V. Thus shalt not kill.

VI. Thou shalt not commit adultery.

VII. Thou shalt not steal.

VIII. Thus shalt not bear false witness.

IX. Thou shalt not covet thy neighbor's wife.

X. Thou shalt not cover the neighbor's goods.

Protestants, on the other hand, number them differently, resulting in the discrepancy:

I. Thou shalt have no strange gods before me.

II. Thou shalt not carve graven images.

III. Thou shalt not take the name of the Lord thy God in vain.

IV. Keep holy the Sabbath.

V. Honor your father and your mother.

VI. Thou shalt not kill.

VII. Thou shalt not commit adultery.

VIII. Thou shalt not steal.

IX. Thou shalt not bear false witness.

X. Thou shalt not covet thy neighbor's wife, and thou shalt not covet thy neighbor's goods.

The first commandment is against idolatry of any kind, including statue worship. So it's senseless to divide it, as Protestants do, into two separate commandments. To worship a graven image as an idol is the exact same sin as "having strange gods" before God himself.

The other discrepancy arises when Protestants incorrectly combine two different sins into a single commandment: "Thou shalt not covet thy neighbor's wife, and thou shalt not covet thy neighbor's goods." The problem here is that coveting your neighbor's wife is in the category of the sin of lust, while coveting his goods is in the category of theft. The Catholic Church condemns as idolatry any form of idol worship or superstition. It also recognizes that there is a legitimate religious use for statues and icons that is not offensive to God. [151]

27. Having religious statues and images, as the Catholic Church does, goes directly against God's command in Exodus 20:4 that we are *not* to carve any graven images of anything. You can't explain away this clear teaching. Catholic statues are really a form of idol worship.

If you look a little closer at Exodus 20:4, you'll see that here God is condemning idolatry, not carving of graven images. The specific graven images He forbade were those that would be worshiped as false gods, but the Lord did *not* forbid making and using religious statues. This is clear in passages such as Exodus 25:18-20, where He commands Moses to carve graven images of angels, which would sit atop the Ark of the Covenant, the most sacred artifact in Israel, aside from the tablets of the Ten Commandments, which the Ark was built to contain. Surely God was not being forgetful. In Exodus 20 He commanded no graven images for the sake of idolatry, but in Exodus 25 He doesn't merely tolerate religious graven images, he *commands* that they be fashioned.

Similarly, we see numerous examples in the Old Testament of God either commanding or approving of religious statues and other graven images. In Numbers 21:8-9, God commanded Moses to fashion the graven image of a serpent so that, in a way known only to God, those Israelites who had been bitten by poisonous seraph serpents in the desert could look upon that statue of a snake that had been held aloft and be healed.[152] This was a legitimate, albeit strangely mysterious, use of a statue. Interestingly, in 2 Kings 18:4, some of the people had begun to slide into idolatry and started worshiping the bronze serpent as a false god. When that happened, King Hezekiah ordered it to be destroyed to prevent idolatry among the people.

In passages such as 1 Kings 6:23-28 and 1 Kings 7:23-29 we see graven images galore in the temple built by King Solomon to honor God: statues and bas-relief friezes of pomegranates, lions, oxen, angels, flower blossoms, and other things were fashioned and placed in profusion throughout the temple. This legitimate use of religious images was in no way contrary to God's law. In fact, in 1 Kings 9:1-3, God specifically approves of the temple and all that was in it, and tells Solomon that He had "consecrated" it, that He had "conferred" His Name upon it forever, and that His "eyes and heart" would "be there always."

If, as you claim, *all* religious statues and images are tantamount to idolatry, how then could God have blessed Solomon's temple for including so many religious images? The answer, of course, is that Solomon's practice of using statues, as with Moses, was not contrary to God's commandment in Exodus 20. The difference was the intention behind it. Carving statues for the purpose of idol worship is to be condemned. Using crucifixes and other religious statues appropriately and without any hint of superstition, to remind us of Christ the Lord and the saints in heaven, whom we can't see with our physical eyes, is completely legitimate. As St. Paul said, we preach Christ crucified (cf. 1 Cor. 1:18, 22-24). And having a crucifix visible is an excellent way to both teach the power of the cross to others as well as for ourselves to remember at what a price our redemption and salvation were obtained.

And consider what the great early Church Father St. John of Damascus[153] said in response to the spurious claim that Catholics worship statues: "We would certainly be in error if we were making an image of the invisible God; for what is incorporeal and invisible and uncircumscribable and without defined figure is not able to be depicted. And again, if we were making images of men and thought them gods, and adored them as gods, certainly we would be impious. But we do not do any of these things."[154]

28. Why does the Catholic Church teach that Mary, the Mother of Jesus, was a "perpetual virgin" when the Bible says she had other children, those known as the "brothers of the Lord" (cf. Matt. 13:55).

Actually, there is no explicit statement in Scripture — not a single one — that Mary had other children besides the Lord, just as there is no explicit statement — not a single one — that says she did *not* have other children. The Bible speaks of the "brothers of the Lord,"[155] At best, we must look for the truth amid the implicit statements in Scripture that can help us know the answer to the question: Was Mary perpetually a virgin?

It's important to keep in mind that there is no argument between Protestants and Catholics regarding the fact that Mary was a virgin before the birth of Christ. The dispute arises over whether she remained that way after His birth.

The Greek word for "brother" is *adelphos*. Not unlike the way the word "brother" is used in modern English, *adelphos* also had a variety of meanings in the New Testament. The literal meaning referred to siblings born of the same mother or father (or both).[156] But *adelphos* was also used in a much wider nonliteral sense, referring, for example, to the first followers of Christ,[157] to any fellow human being,[158] to one's fellow countrymen,[159] to friends, extended family, and neighbors,[160] and also to fellow Christians.[161] This is an important biblical clue to keep in mind. It would be a serious mistake to assume that just because a man is called the "brother" (*adelphos*) of the Lord that it means that he was a son of Mary the mother of Jesus. Depending on the context in which we see it used, the word *adelphos* can indeed have the connotation of a sibling (i.e., from the same womb), but it does not always mean that. In fact, in both the Old and New Testaments, it frequently does *not* mean that.

Perhaps the most intriguing passage pertaining to this issue is Matthew 13:55-56, where four men are named as the "brothers" (Greek: *adelphoi*) of Christ: James, Joseph, Simon, and Judas.[162] For those who believe that Mary did not remain a virgin after Christ's birth, in other words, that she had normal marital relations with St. Joseph during the rest of their marriage, this passage seems to cinch the case against the Catholic teaching on Mary's perpetual virginity. But in reality, it really doesn't in the least disprove it. The reason is that two of these four men who are called Christ's "brothers," James[163] and Joseph, were actually the sons of another Mary — the wife of Cleophas.[164] This relationship can be seen by comparing Matthew 27:56 with John 19:25 and Mark 15:40-47; 16:1.

This very clearly indicates that just because these men were known as the "brothers" of the Lord, at least two of them, James and Joseph, were not the sons of Mary, the mother of Jesus. Christian Tradition since the earliest years upheld and affirmed the consistent teaching that Mary was a perpetual virgin.

29. I believe in the Virgin Birth, but I find it very difficult, if not impossible, to imagine that Mary had no other children besides Jesus. It would not have been normal for Mary and Joseph not to have pro-created other children together.

I think it's safe to say that there was nothing at all "normal" about the way God chose Mary, a virgin, to become the mother of the Incarnate Second Person of the Trinity. There was nothing normal about God delivering this staggering news through the message of an angel, or reassuring St. Joseph to marry her through a dream. And the Holy Family was certainly not normal when compared with any other family. Your son might be an honor student or the school's spelling-bee champ or the captain of the basketball team, but *their* Son was God himself. So you see, to argue that it wouldn't have been "normal" for Mary and Joseph not to have had other children misses the reality of the situation: Nothing about it was normal.

This means that we cannot expect that things were done according to what is, by our standards, "normal." Rather, God's plan for Joseph and Mary was arranged according to what was fitting, in light of their unique circumstances. And Mary remaining true to a vow of virginity would have been far more fitting than for her to have had other children, after God himself had inhabited her womb. As God himself said: "For my thoughts are not your thoughts, neither are your ways my ways, says the LORD. For as the heavens are higher than the earth, so are my ways higher than your ways and my thoughts than your thoughts."[165]

The most likely, even certain, reason for Mary not having other children is that she had made a vow of perpetual virginity when she was a girl. Such things were not common, but they also were not unheard of.[166] St. Augustine commented on this, saying, "Mary answered the announcing angel: 'How shall this be done, because I know not man?' She would not have said this unless she had already vowed her virginity to God."[167]

Here's another key piece of biblical evidence that will help us draw the proper conclusion. It revolves around the two episodes in which the Angel Gabriel is sent by God to deliver important tidings, first to Zechariah, the father of St. John the Baptist; second to Mary, who would become the Mother of Christ. Look at what happens in the first passage:

> Now while he [Zechariah] was serving as priest before God when his division was on duty, according to the custom of the priesthood, it fell to him by lot to enter the temple of the Lord and burn incense.

And the whole multitude of the people were praying outside at the hour of incense. And there appeared to him an angel of the Lord standing on the right side of the altar of incense.

And Zechariah was troubled when he saw him, and fear fell upon him. But the angel said to him, "Do not be afraid, Zechariah, for your prayer is heard, and your wife Elizabeth will bear you a son, and you shall call his name John. And you will have joy and gladness, and many will rejoice at his birth; for he will be great before the Lord, and he shall drink no wine nor strong drink, and he will be filled with the Holy Spirit, even from his mother's womb. And he will turn many of the sons of Israel to the Lord their God, and he will go before him in the spirit and power of Elijah, to turn the hearts of the fathers to the children, and the disobedient to the wisdom of the just, to make ready for the Lord a people prepared."

And Zechariah said to the angel, "How shall I know this? For I am an old man, and my wife is advanced in years."

And the angel answered him, "I am Gabriel, who stand in the presence of God; and I was sent to speak to you, and to bring you this good news. And behold, you will be silent and unable to speak until the day that these things come to pass, because you did not believe my words, which will be fulfilled in their time."

And the people were waiting for Zechariah, and they wondered at his delay in the temple. And when he came out, he could not speak to them, and they perceived that he had seen a vision in the temple; and he made signs to them and remained dumb. (Luke 1:8-22)

Now compare that passage with Luke 1:26-38 for an important parallel:

And in the sixth month, the angel Gabriel was sent from God into a city of Galilee, called Nazareth, to a virgin espoused to a man whose name was Joseph, of the house of David: and the virgin's name was Mary.

And the angel being come in, said unto her: "Hail, full of grace, the Lord is with thee: blessed art thou among women."

[Mary, who] having heard, was troubled at his saying and thought with herself what manner of salutation this should be.

And the angel said to her: "Fear not, Mary, for thou hast found grace with God. Behold thou shalt conceive in thy womb and shalt bring forth a son: and thou shalt call his name Jesus. He shall be great and shall be called the Son of the Most High. And the Lord God shall give unto him the throne of David his father: and he shall reign in the house of Jacob forever. And of his kingdom there shall be no end."

And Mary said to the angel, "How shall this be done, because I know not man?"

And the angel answering, said to her, "The Holy Ghost shall come upon thee and the power of the Most High shall overshadow thee. And therefore also the Holy which shall be born of thee shall be called the Son of God. And behold thy cousin Elizabeth, she also hath conceived a son in her old age: and this is the sixth month with her that is called barren. Because no word shall be impossible with God."

And Mary said, "Behold the handmaid of the Lord: be it done to me according to thy word."

And the angel departed from her.[168]

Notice that in the first passage, Zachariah "was troubled" by the Angel's message, just as Mary was when she received hers. Zachariah responded, saying, "How shall I know this? For I am an old man, and my wife is advanced in years." Mary's response was almost identical in tone: " 'How can this be, since I have no husband [I know not man]?' " In other words, both Zachariah and Mary both doubted the angel, but notice that only Zachariah was punished for that! He was rebuked and struck dumb as his punishment. But Mary was neither rebuked nor punished. Why?

The answer to this points us to Mary's perpetual virginity.

And finally, consider these two additional scriptural evidences that point to Mary's perpetual virginity. The first is the episode when the Holy Family went up to Jerusalem when the Christ Child was about thirteen-years-old (Luke 2:41-52). If Mary had other children after Christ, where are they? None are mentioned. The Holy Family is described as simply his parents and the Lord himself, without even the slightest suggestion that there were other children.

The second incident in Scripture that points us to — though it certainly does not prove — the Catholic teaching that Mary was a perpetual virgin, is the crucifixion. Here we see Mary standing at the foot of the cross. Alongside her were several other holy women, as well as St. John the Apostle. When he is about to die, the Lord looks down from the cross:

"When Jesus saw his mother, and the disciple whom he loved standing near, he said to his mother, 'Woman, behold, your son!' Then he said to the disciple, 'Behold, your mother!' And from that hour the disciple took her to his own home" (John 19:26-27).

Why would Christ entrust his own mother into the care of a man who was not a member of the family if indeed Mary had other sons and daughters besides Christ? He wouldn't have. If Mary had actually had other children, she would have gone to live with them. The fact that Christ entrusted his Mother to St. John is a strong indication that Mary had no other children.

30. Catholics have departed from the pure light of biblical truth on the subject of Mary's so-called

perpetual virginity. I thank God for the Protestant Reformation that recovered the biblical truth on this and so many other Christian teachings that the Catholic Church has distorted and/or rejected.

You seem to be blissfully unaware that Martin Luther and John Calvin — the progenitors of two of the three major branches of the Protestant Reformation — both held firmly to this Catholic teaching. So I'd ask you to consider the following pertinent quotes from these two Protestant leaders. I'd also respectfully ask our Fundamentalist and Evangelical friends who read these statements by Luther and Calvin, et al., to think carefully about them and consider just how far modern-day Protestantism has drifted from its 16th-century moorings. More importantly, ponder how very far modern Protestantism has drifted from the fifteen centuries of the historic Catholic Faith that preceded the Protestant Reformation.

Martin Luther — "When Matthew [1:25] says that Joseph did not know Mary carnally until she had brought forth her son, it does not follow that he knew her subsequently; on the contrary, it means that he never did know her."[169]

"He, Christ, our Savior, was the real and natural fruit of Mary's virginal womb. . . . This was without the cooperation of a man, and she remained a virgin after that."[170]

"[Mary is] the highest woman and the noblest gem in Christianity after Christ. . . . She is nobility, wisdom, and holiness personified. We can never honor her enough."[171]

"It is a sweet and pious belief that the infusion of Mary's soul was effected without original sin; so that in the very infusion of her soul she was also purified from original sin and adorned with God's gifts, receiving a pure soul infused by God? Thus from the first moment she began to live she was free from all sin."

"Christ, our Savior, was the real and natural fruit of Mary's virginal womb . . . this was without the cooperation of a man, and she remained a virgin after that."[172]

"Christ . . . was the only Son of Mary, and the Virgin Mary bore no children besides Him. . . . I am inclined to agree with those who declare that 'brothers' really mean 'cousins' here, for Holy Writ and the Jews always call cousins brothers."[173]

"A new lie about me is being circulated. I am supposed to have preached and written that Mary, the mother of God, was not a virgin either before or after the birth of Christ . . ."[174]

John Calvin — "It cannot be denied that God in choosing and destining Mary to be the Mother of his Son, granted her the highest honor. . . . Elizabeth called Mary Mother of the Lord, because the unity of the person in the two natures of Christ was such that she could have said that the mortal man engendered in the womb of Mary was at the same time the eternal God."[175]

"There have been certain folk who have wished to suggest from this passage [i.e., Matt. 1:25] that the

Virgin Mary had other children than the Son of God, and that Joseph had then dwelt with her later; but what folly this is! For the gospel writer did not wish to record what happened afterwards; he simply wished to make clear Joseph's obedience and to show also that Joseph had been well and truly assured that it was God who had sent His angel to Mary. He had therefore never dwelt with her nor had he shared her company. . . . And besides this Our Lord Jesus Christ is called the first born. This is not because there was a second or a third, but because the gospel writer is paying regard to precedence. Scripture speaks thus of naming the first-born whether or not there was any question of the second."[176]

Ulrich Zwingli — "I firmly believe that Mary, according to the words of the gospel as a pure Virgin brought forth for us the Son of God and in childbirth and after childbirth forever remained a pure, intact Virgin."[177]

31. You Catholics are obsessed with Mary's perpetual virginity. Why don't you just concentrate on Jesus and forget about her?

Obsessed? No. At least no more so than Martin Luther or John Calvin were when they said what they said above about that doctrine. And let's not forget that Catholic Marian teachings are always at the forefront of the arguments that are consistently raised by Protestant critics of the Catholic Church. So, since it always seems to get around to Mary in discussions about religion between Catholics and Protestants (as well as Jehovah's Witnesses and Mormons), why do you object when a Catholic raises the issue first? Is there an unspoken double standard at work here, perhaps? The fact is, the belief in Mary's perpetual virginity was universal and consistent within Christianity in the fifteen centuries prior to the Protestant Reformation. In proclaiming Mary's special status, no Christian, including Martin Luther and John Calvin, is somehow "robbing" Christ when they acknowledge her perpetual virginity.

In the same way that Christ is not "robbed" of glory when we admire and praise a beautiful sunset or a mountain, neither is He robbed of glory or honor when we venerate Mary and the saints, whether for her perpetual virginity or for any attribute they possessed. For after all, any good thing we have comes from God.

Catholics are not "obsessed" with Mary's perpetual virginity. Rather, we are careful to preserve the deposit of faith that has been "once for all delivered to the saints" (Jude 3), and that deposit of faith has always included the teaching that Mary remained a virgin her entire life. To proclaim and defend that truth does not equate with "obsession" any more than proclaiming and defending the Trinity, or the Eucharist, or the divinity of Christ, would be an obsession. The truth is the truth, and proclaiming it is always important, whether it's a central truth, such as the Trinity or the divinity of Christ, or a truth of lesser magnitude, such as the virginity of Mary. Since the truth is an organic whole, each part of the truth is inextricably bound up with all the other parts. And so to downplay, devalue, or deny the truth about Mary's role in God's plan of salvation is to weaken one's grasp of the entire body of revealed truth. Conversely, to proclaim any individual facet of truth is to uphold the whole truth.

To borrow from the analogy of a body that St. Paul used in 1 Corinthians 12:14-26, we can think about revealed truth like a body. Each part of that truth, or doctrine, whether a vital organ such as the heart or a more peripheral part, such as an ear or a foot, is important to the unity and integrity of the whole body. So, too, with Mary's perpetual virginity.

32. Why do Catholics violate the Lord's command not to engage in "vain repetition" when praying (Matt. 6:7)? The Rosary and other Catholic formula prayers are clearly repetitious and condemned by the Bible.

Jesus said, "And in praying do not heap up empty phrases as the Gentiles do; for they think that they will be heard for their many words" (Matt. 6:7). He warns about the "empty phrases" of the Gentiles not because they repeated them, but because the false gods to whom they prayed didn't exist. That's why all their "many words" were vain and useless. But the Bible nowhere prohibits the practice of praying formula prayers repeatedly. In fact, it proves just the opposite.

In Matthew 26:39, 42, 44, for example, we read that the Lord himself repeated the same prayer three times: "And going a little farther he fell on his face and prayed, 'My Father, if it be possible, let this cup pass from me; nevertheless, not as I will, but as thou wilt. . . .' "

> Again, for the second time, he went away and prayed, "My Father, if this cannot pass unless I drink it, thy will be done. . . ."
>
> So, leaving them again, he went away and prayed for the third time, saying the same words.

Psalm 136 is another example of a God-honoring repetitious prayer. The refrain "for his steadfast love endures for ever" is repeated many times. In fact, the Holy Spirit inspired this prayer for us to pray! Ask yourself this question: Why would the Holy Spirit inspire the writer of the psalms to repeat this prayer if Christ was condemning repetition in Matthew 6? That wouldn't make any sense (besides, it would be contrary to God's nature to have division between the Second and Third Persons of the Blessed Trinity).[178]

And finally, keep in mind that what made the pagan's prayers "vain" was not the fact that they were repeated. Rather, it was because the gods they were praying to didn't exist. No matter how much they repeated their invocations, it was pointless because Zeus, or Apollo, or Diana, weren't there to hear them. And while it's true that Christ was warning us to avoid any semblance of mechanical, mindless, repetitious prayer mantras, because they are cheap imitations of real, from-the-heart prayer, He wasn't condemning the repetition of prayer altogether. After all, when people asked Jesus to teach them how to pray, He didn't say, "Avoid repetitious prayers and just say what comes into your mind." Instead, He taught them the greatest prayer of all, the Our Father. He said that when we pray, we are to pray "like this."

Authentic Christian prayer, such as that found in the prayers, hymns, and liturgies of the Catholic Church, is never simply "heaping up empty phrases." It is rather relying on the truth and beauty embodied in those prayers as a way to unite ourselves more closely with God, ask for mercy, intercede for ourselves and others, and above all, to thank and praise Him with all our hearts. I hope you'll agree that, if anything is worth repeating, it would be a prayer that honors and praises God and His saints.

33. Catholics are confused about what biblical worship really is. You claim you only give Mary and the saints and angels "honor," not worship, but in reality you really do worship them. Any sort of praying to, praising, or bowing to, any human being is worship, whether you call it that or not. How can you deny this?

Actually, I'll let the Bible do the denying for me. It's much easier that way. Your argument fails because it doesn't take into account what the Bible really says about "honoring," "praising," and "bowing down before" fellow human beings or angels. Let's start with the act of bowing before another human being to show honor and reverence — which is exactly what Catholics intend to show the saints: honor and reverence, or, as it is also called, veneration.

Bowing Down

The Bible is clear that we must never "bow down to" and worship any creature in the way only God may be worshiped (i.e., adoration) — Exodus 20:5 being a prime example of this prohibition. But if our intention is not to do that, it is permissible to bow down before a fellow creature to give homage. In fact, the Hebrew word for "to bow down to" someone is "*shachah*." It appears in Exodus 20:5, where we are forbidden to commit idolatry, as well as in passages such as Genesis 27:29, where it is permitted, even good, to bow down before a creature to show honor and veneration.

Consider these biblical examples of bowing down before fellow creatures:

> And the LORD appeared to [Abraham] by the oaks of Mamre, as he sat at the door of his tent in the heat of the day. He lifted up his eyes and looked, and behold, three men stood in front of

him. When he saw them, he ran from the tent door to meet them, and bowed himself to the earth, and said, "My lord, if I have found favor in your sight, do not pass by your servant. Let a little water be brought, and wash your feet, and rest yourselves under the tree, while I fetch a morsel of bread, that you may refresh yourselves, and after that you may pass on — since you have come to your servant." So they said, "Do as you have said." (Gen. 18:1-5)

The context of this mysterious passage indicates that Abraham most likely had no idea who these three men were. It seems that he understood them to be angels who had been sent by God. And yet he bowed down before them as a sign of honor and reverence. This seems the most plausible explanation based on the text, especially in light of verses 21 and 22: "[The Lord said] 'I will go down to see whether they have done altogether according to the outcry which has come to me; and if not, I will know.' So the men turned from there, and went toward Sodom; but Abraham still stood before the LORD." If the three men "turned from there" and headed away, yet Abraham was still standing before the Lord, he almost certainly did not regard those three as manifestations (a theophany of the Blessed Trinity, perhaps?) of God, but as his angels.

Then his father Isaac said to him, "Come near and kiss me, my son." . . . May God give you of

> the dew of heaven, and of the fatness of the earth, and plenty of grain and wine. Let peoples serve you, and nations bow down to you. Be lord over your brothers, and may your mother's sons bow down to you." (Gen. 27:29)

In light of this verse in which the holy Patriarch Isaac invokes a sacred ritual blessing upon his son, asking God to make others bow in honor before him, it's difficult to the point of being impossible to imagine that bowing and giving honor to a fellow human being — when done appropriately and with the correct intention — could possibly be contrary to God's law.

> When Joshua was by Jericho, he lifted up his eyes and looked, and behold, a man stood before him with his drawn sword in his hand; and Joshua went to him and said to him, "Are you for us, or for our adversaries?" And he said, "No; but as commander of the army of the LORD I have now come." And Joshua fell on his face to the earth, and worshiped, and said to him, "What does my lord bid his servant?" And the commander of the LORD's army said to Joshua, "Put off your shoes from your feet; for the place where you stand is holy." And Joshua did so. (Josh. 5:13-15)

Here we see an angel, perhaps St. Michael the Archangel, conversing with Joshua. Notice two things: First, that this holy leader of God's people bows down in homage (and fear!) before this creature, and second, that the angel doesn't rebuke him for doing so. Why? Because it was clear that Joshua wasn't giving worship to the angel, something reserved to God alone, as Joshua well knew. Rather, he was showing appropriate honor.

Compare this passage with what happened when St. John bowed before an angel in the Book of Revelation (19:10)[179] and you'll see that the intention behind the act of bowing down to give honor is all-important. Joshua didn't intend to worship the angel he met. John, amazingly, did. And he was justifiably rebuked for it. Now look at these other passages:

> Then Boaz said to Ruth, "Now, listen, my daughter, do not go to glean in another field or leave this one, but keep close to my maidens. Let your eyes be upon the field which they are reaping, and go after them. Have I not charged the young men not to molest you? And when you are thirsty, go to the vessels and drink what the young men have drawn." Then she fell on her face, bowing to the ground, and said to him, "Why have I found favor in your eyes, that you should take notice of me, when I am a foreigner?" But Boaz answered her, "All that you have done for your mother-in-law since the death of your husband has been fully told me, and how you left your father and mother and your native land and came to a people that you did not know before. The LORD recompense you for what you have

done, and a full reward be given you by the LORD, the God of Israel, under whose wings you have come to take refuge!" (Ruth 2:8-12)

Afterward David also arose, and went out of the cave, and called after Saul, "My lord the king!" And when Saul looked behind him, David bowed with his face to the earth, and did obeisance. (1 Sam. 24:8)

Rising and bowing to the ground, she answered, "Your handmaid would become a slave to wash the feet of my lord's servants." (1 Sam. 25:41)

So Bathsheba went to the king into his chamber (now the king was very old, and Abishag the Shunammite was ministering to the king). Bathsheba bowed and did obeisance to the king, and the king said, "What do you desire?" (1 Kings 1:15-16)

While she was still speaking with the king, Nathan the prophet came in. And they told the king, "Here is Nathan the prophet." And when he came in before the king, he bowed before the king, with his face to the ground.[180] (1 Kings 1:22-24)

When the man of God saw her coming. . . . When Elisha came into the house, he saw the child lying dead on his bed. So he went in and shut the door upon the two of them, and prayed to the

Lord. Then he went up and lay upon the child, putting his mouth upon his mouth, his eyes upon his eyes, and his hands upon his hands; and as he stretched himself upon him, the flesh of the child became warm. Then he got up again, and walked once to and fro in the house, and went up, and stretched himself upon him; the child sneezed seven times, and the child opened his eyes. Then he summoned Gehazi and said, "Call this Shunammite." So he called her. And when she came to him, he said, "Take up your son." She came and fell at his feet, bowing to the ground; then she took up her son and went out. (2 Kings 4:25-37)

Then David said to all the assembly, "Bless the Lord your God." And all the assembly blessed the Lord, the God of their fathers, and bowed their heads, and worshiped the Lord, and did obeisance to the king. [181] (1 Chron. 29:20)

So the servant fell on his knees, imploring him, "Lord, have patience with me, and I will pay you everything." (Matt. 18:26)

"[To the church at Philadelphia] I know your works. Behold, I have set before you an open door, which no one is able to shut; I know that you have but little power, and yet you have kept my word and have not denied my name. Behold, I will make those of the synagogue of Satan who say that they are Jews and are not, but lie — behold, I will make them come and bow down before your feet, and learn that I have loved you." (Rev. 3:8-9)

You are really arguing not with the Catholic Church on this issue so much as with Jesus Christ himself, for it is He who says He will compel people to give honor to His followers, the saints, even by bowing down to them.[182]

And here's a final point I'd ask you to ponder prayerfully. We know that Jesus Christ, who is God himself, is the "King of Kings,"[183] and yet, as we've seen above, he permits mere human kings to receive honor and veneration from their subjects. For example, the Bible says in 1 Kings 15:22 and 15:28-37 that it was not only permissible but appropriate for people to bow down, do homage to, and venerate the person of the king, even though he was a mere human being.

So on what biblical basis do you assert that, once these holy men and women enter into heaven, that they are somehow no longer able to receive veneration and honor as they did on earth? The truth is, there is no biblical basis for such an assertion.

Or to put it a different way, since the Lord God is not displeased that human beings, such as the monarch in 1 Kings 15, receive homage and veneration while here on earth, while they are imperfect and sinful, what changes once they die? Now that they are "just men made perfect" (Heb. 12:23) and reign with God in glory in heaven as kings and queens, why would

God do a 180-degree turn on this issue and suddenly forbid that these saints should receive honor and veneration now that they are in heaven? Does that idea make sense to you? Of course not. The truth is, if God permitted and even approved of venerating holy men and women here on earth, it makes no sense whatsoever, nor is there any biblical warrant to suppose, that He should somehow not approve of honoring and venerating them now that they are in heaven.

34. Even though Romanists pray to Mary and the so-called saints, the early Christians knew nothing of such theological stupidity. They prayed to God alone. It wasn't until the Dark Ages that Catholic superstition and idolatry surrounding Mary sprang up like a weed to choke off the truth.

Well, if nothing else, I'll give you an "A" for providing us with a colorful, if not incorrect, argument. The fact is, the early Christians did indeed invoke the intercession of Mary and the saints through prayer. For example, the earliest extant prayer to Mary is the "*Sub Tuum Praesidium*,"[184] which dates back to at least the early 200s, perhaps even earlier. This example of Christian prayer from the early Church deflates your contention that early Christians didn't seek Mary's intercession:

> Beneath your protection we fly, O Holy
> Mother of God. In our necessities, despise not

our petitions but always deliver us from all dangers, oh glorious blessed Virgin.

Keep in mind that this prayer, as with all other early Christian invocations of Mary and the saints, was not a prayer of worship. It was a prayer asking for intercession. This is rooted in a biblical principle expressed by St. Paul:

> I urge that supplications, prayers, intercessions, and thanksgivings be made for all men, for kings and all who are in high positions, that we may lead a quiet and peaceable life, godly and respectful in every way. This is good, and it is acceptable in the sight of God our Savior. (1 Tim. 2:1-4)

When the early Christians invoked Mary's intercession, they were simply following St. Paul's teaching. For, as one of the blessed in heaven, she remains just as much a member of the Body of Christ now as she was when she was alive on this earth. And that means that her heavenly "supplications, prayers, intercessions, and thanksgivings" before the Blessed Trinity are "good and acceptable in the sight of God our savior."

The testimony of the early Church is important to note here:

> "Remember me, you heirs of God, you brethren of Christ; supplicate the Savior earnestly for me, that I may be freed through Christ from him

that fights against me day by day"[185] (St. Ephraim the Syrian, A.D. 370).

You victorious martyrs who endured torments gladly for the sake of the God and Savior, you who have boldness of speech toward the Lord himself, you saints, intercede for us who are timid and sinful men, full of sloth, that the grace of Christ may come upon us, and enlighten the hearts of all of us that so we may love him.[186] (St. Ephraim the Syrian, A.D. 370)

By the command of your only-begotten Son we communicate with the memory of your saints . . . by whose prayers and supplications have mercy upon us all, and deliver us for the sake of your holy name.[187] (St. Basil the Great, A.D. 373)

In the early centuries of the Church, that Mary and the saints can and do pray for us, and that we can and should invoke their intercession, was widely recognized and believed. The Catholic Church — which is that original Church — continues to proclaim that biblical truth.

35. How can Mary or any saint in heaven possibly hear all the prayers from Catholics all over the world, offering prayers and petitions in many different languages simultaneously? That would require omniscience and omnipresence, two attributes of God alone!

Actually, no. Mary would not need to be either omniscient of omnipresent to hear all those prayers, no matter how many people were praying at any one time. The reason is that omniscience and omnipresence are attributes of God that mean endless, infinite knowledge and presence. But no matter how many prayers there are at any given moment, it still is a finite amount. So Mary, a creature, could be able to be aware of them. The real difficulty for you and me in trying to understand *how* this could be is that here on earth our abilities are paltry compared to the abilities the blessed in heaven enjoy.[188] Which means that just because we can't mentally cope with even three different people speaking to us simultaneously, much less millions of them, doesn't mean that the blessed in heaven, with their vastly enhanced, glorified and perfected human natures,[189] can't.

Think of it this way: A one-year old baby has a very limited ability to communicate and process information. She can't talk, she can't understand complex or abstract speech, and she can't reason. At least not when she's a year old. But-fast forward 30 years now to when she's a young woman. Now she has an enormously greater ability to communicate, reason, and process complex information. While it would be completely impossible for her, when she was a baby, to understand even basic math concepts such as two plus two equals four, by the time she becomes a young woman, she may well have learned algebra, trigonometry, calculus, and other advanced forms of math. So you see, just because a baby isn't capable of that mental effort does not imply that the woman would also be incapable. And the same is true of Mary and the saints, as well as the angels (who are also creatures, as we are). While on earth, Mary and the saints couldn't do many of the amazing things they now can do in heaven. As the writer of Hebrews said, in heaven we will find "the spirits of the just *made perfect.*"[190] We may not understand how they can hear our prayers, but we know they can. In fact, Jesus himself makes this point quite clear:

> "Just so, I tell you, there will be more joy in heaven over one sinner who repents than over ninety-nine righteous persons who need no repentance. . . . Just so, I tell you, there is joy before the angels of God over one sinner who repents." (Luke 15:7-10)

St. Paul also reminds us in 1 Corinthians 13:8-13, right now, in this mortal stage of our lives, our knowledge is imperfect and we can only see "dimly." But when we get to heaven, our ability to understand, see, and know will be immeasurably enhanced.[191] Remember that these amazing gifts of power and knowledge that God bestows on His saints are *gifts*. As St. Bonaventure once wrote, He shares these gifts with us "not to *increase* His glory, but to show it forth and communicate it."[192] This is a key to understanding that the saints in heaven can indeed hear our prayers of petition and respond by interceding before the throne of God on our behalf.

And another biblical truth for you to consider which, I hope, will make you reconsider your objection to this Catholic (and I would add, biblical) teaching, is that the Bible tells us that the devil himself has a vast ability to tempt, harass, and even harm the billions of people on this earth.[193] In 1 Peter 5:8, St. Peter says that Satan is like a "roaring lion" who prowls around the world searching for people to devour. St. Peter tells us to be vigilant and "resist him." What this means is, although he is a creature and is neither omniscient nor omnipresent, the devil can still operate in the spiritual realm in a way far beyond our understanding. Somehow, at any given moment, he is able to tempt millions of people in various cultures speaking various languages. Though he is just a creature, he is somehow able to roam around, looking to spiritually "devour" large numbers of people: hundreds, thousands, even millions, at any given moment. Does he need to be omniscient or omnipresent to do this? No. Can he do these things? Yes, the Bible is clear that he can. So the issue really becomes: If even Satan, a twisted, evil, corrupted fallen angel, can do these amazing things that defy our understanding, *how much more* so can those righteous, grace-filled, spiritually perfected, friends of Christ (Mary and the saints) hear and understand our prayers and petition the Lord on our behalf![194]

Somehow, in a way known only to God, those in heaven — i.e., Mary, the saints, and the angels — can know about even individual acts of repentance here on earth. This means that they somehow are able to process that information. We may not know how they do it, but it is foolish, not to mention unbiblical, to deny that they *can* do it.

36. I believe it's wrong to call Mary the "Mother of God." She was only the mother of His human nature, not His divinity. There's no way that the eternal God could have a "mother."

You might believe it's wrong to honor Mary with the title "Mother of God," but you're out of step with two thousand years of historic Christian teaching on this issue. The early Church Fathers, the early Councils, and the constant teaching of the Church, has been that the title "Mother of God" is both appropriate and accurate in describing the Blessed Virgin Mary's unique and exalted role among God's creatures. She was chosen to carry in her womb for nine months, give birth to, and raise into adulthood Jesus Christ — God himself.

Keep in mind that women don't give birth to a nature, they give birth to a person. When your mom gave birth to you, she didn't show you off to your family and friends saying, "Oh look at the new *nature* we have in our family." She introduced you as a *person.* And in the Incarnation,[195] when God the Son, for our salvation, took human nature and was born among us, He was one person (God) with two natures (divine and human). The person who was born at the Nativity was God himself. Mary is His mother. It's an astounding concept, but it's true, even so. Consider what these early Church Fathers said on the subject:

> The Virgin Mary, being obedient to his word, received from an angel the glad tidings that she would bear God. (*Against Heresies*, 5:19:1, St. Irenaeus of Lyons, A.D. 189)

> [T]o all generations they [the prophets] have pictured forth the grandest subjects for contemplation and for action. Thus, too, they preached of the advent of God in the flesh to the world, His advent by the spotless and God-bearing (Greek: *Theotokos*) Mary in the way of birth and growth, and the manner of His life and conversation with men, and His manifestation by baptism, and the new birth that was to be to all men, and the regeneration by the laver [of baptism]. (*Discourse on the End of the World*, 1, St. Hippolytus, A.D. 217)

> For Luke, in the inspired Gospel narratives, delivers a testimony not to Joseph only, but also to Mary the Mother of God, and gives this

account with reference to the very family and house of David. (*Four Homilies,* 1, St. Gregory Thaumaturges, A.D. 262)

Hail to thee for ever, you virgin Mother of God, our unceasing joy, for unto thee do I again return. . . . Hail, you fount of the Son's love for man. . . . Wherefore, we pray thee, the most excellent among women, who boasts in the confidence of your maternal honors, that you would unceasingly keep us in remembrance. O holy Mother of God, remember us, I say, who make our boast in thee, and who in hymns august celebrate the memory, which will ever live, and never fade away. (*ibid.,* 14, St. Methodius, A.D. 305)

We acknowledge the resurrection of the dead, of which Jesus Christ our Lord became the firstling; he bore a body not in appearance but in truth derived from Mary the Mother of God. *(Letter to All Non-Egyptian Bishops*, 12, St. Alexander of Alexandria, A.D. 324)

The Father bears witness from heaven to his Son. The Holy Spirit bears witness, coming down bodily in the form of a dove. The Archangel Gabriel bears witness, bringing the good tidings to Mary. The Virgin Mother of God bears witness. (*Catechetical Lectures*, 10:19, St. Cyril of Jerusalem, A.D. 350)

Though still a virgin she carried a child in her womb, and the handmaid and work of his wisdom became the Mother of God. *(Songs of Praise, 1:20, St. Ephraim the Syrian, A.D. 351)*

The Word begotten of the Father from on high, inexpressibly, inexplicably, incomprehensibly, and eternally, is he that is born in time here below of the Virgin Mary, the Mother of God. *(The Incarnation of the Word of God, 8, St. Athanasius, A.D. 365)*

Being perfect at the side of the Father and incarnate among us, not in appearance but in truth, he [Christ] reshaped man to perfection in himself from Mary the Mother of God through the Holy Spirit. *(The Man Well-Anchored, 75, St. Epiphanius of Salamis, A.D. 374)*

The first thing which kindles ardor in learning is the greatness of the teacher. What is greater than the Mother of God? What more glorious than she whom glory itself chose? *(The Virgins, 2:2, St. Ambrose of Milan, A.D. 377)*

If anyone does not agree that Holy Mary is Mother of God, he is at odds with the Godhead. *(Letter to Cledonius the Priest, 101, St. Gregory Nazianzen, A.D. 382)*

As to how a virgin became the Mother of God, he [Rufinius] has full knowledge; as to how he himself was born, he knows nothing. (*Against Rufinus*, 2:10, St. Jerome, A.D. 401)

Do not marvel at the novelty of the thing, if a Virgin gives birth to *God*. (*Commentaries on Isaiah*, 3:7:15, St. Jerome, A.D. 409)

When, therefore, they ask, "Is Mary mother of man or Mother of God?" we answer, "Both!" The one by the very nature of what was done and the other by relation. Mother of man because it was a man who was in the womb of Mary and who came forth from there, and the Mother of God because God was in the man who was born. (*The Incarnation*, 15, Theodore of Mopsuestia, A.D. 405)

If those representative quotes from the Fathers showing the early Church firmly believed in Mary as the "Mother of God" don't give you pause, at least ponder the words of Mary's cousin, Elizabeth, who greeted her saying, "Blessed are you among women, and blessed is the fruit of your womb!

And why is this granted me, that *the mother of my Lord* should come to me?" (Luke 1:42-43). As you can see, Mary was not the mother of the nature of the Lord; she is acknowledged as the mother of the *Lord*, who is God himself.

THE SAINTS

37. Those in heaven are oblivious to what's happening here on earth. Jesus said that in heaven they will be at rest. So it's foolish for Catholics to imagine that the saints are busy up there worrying about your problems.

The saints are at rest, true, but they are also aware (to the extent God permits) of what's happening here on earth. The easiest example of this is found in the Book of Revelation 6: 9-11, where we see the martyrs beneath the altar of God:

> When he opened the fifth seal, I saw under the altar the souls of those who had been slain for the word of God and for the witness they had borne; they cried out with a loud voice, "O Sovereign Lord, holy and true, how long before thou wilt judge and avenge our blood on those who dwell upon the earth?" Then they were each given a white robe and told to rest a little longer, until the number of their fellow servants and their brethren should be complete, who were to be killed as they themselves had been.

> And after six days Jesus took with him Peter and James and John his brother, and led them up a high mountain apart. And he was transfigured before them, and his face shone like the sun, and

THE SAINTS

his garments became white as light. And behold, there appeared to them Moses and Elijah, talking with him. And Peter said to Jesus, "Lord, it is well that we are here; if you wish, I will make three booths here, one for you and one for Moses and one for Elijah." He was still speaking, when lo, a bright cloud overshadowed them, and a voice from the cloud said, "This is my beloved Son, with whom I am well pleased; listen to him." (Matt. 17:1-5)

Here are other verses[196] that show the "dead" who are in heaven are quite awake and aware:

"And as for the dead being raised, have you not read in the book of Moses, in the passage about the bush, how God said to him, 'I am the God of Abraham, and the God of Isaac, and the God of Jacob'? He is not God of the dead, but of the living; you are quite wrong."[197] (Mark 12:26-27)

Therefore, since we are surrounded by so great a cloud of witnesses, let us also lay aside every weight, and sin which clings so closely, and let us run with perseverance the race that is set before us, looking to Jesus the pioneer and perfecter of our faith, who for the joy that was set before him endured the cross, despising the shame, and is seated at the right hand of the throne of God. . . . But you have come to Mount Zion and to the city of the living God, the heavenly Jerusalem, and to innumerable angels in festal gathering, and to the assembly of the first-born who are enrolled in heaven, and to a judge who is God of all, and to the spirits of just men made perfect. (Heb. 12:1-2, 22-23)[198]

THE MAGISTERIUM

38. I have no need of the Catholic Church and its alleged "magisterium" to teach me anything. I have God's Word, which is sufficient for me. The Bible says, "But the anointing which ye have received of him abideth in you, and ye need not that any man teach you" (1 John 2:27, King James Version).

You may not think you have need of the magisterium, but Jesus Christ knows you do. That's why He established His Church to "teach all nations" all those things that He commands us to believe (cf. Matt. 20:19-20). What's interesting about the passage you quoted is that in that very context, St. John was teaching the Christians through his inspired epistle. If in an absolute sense his audience needed no one to teach them anything, then why did the Holy Spirit inspire St. John to teach them what he taught them in that epistle? What's more, if Christians don't need teachers, then why did the Lord establish in the Church the office of teacher?

He who descended is he who also ascended far above all the heavens, that he might fill all things. And his gifts were that some should be apostles, some prophets, some evangelists, some pastors and *teachers*, to equip the saints for the work of ministry, for building up the body of Christ. (Eph. 4:10-12)

The fact is, you do need teachers. We all do. What St. John meant in that passage is somewhat obscure, but we can at least rule out that he didn't literally mean we don't need teachers, otherwise the passages above would be gibberish.

39. I'm a nondenominational Christian. I don't need a Church to tell me how to follow Jesus Christ. I have the Bible, and that's all I need. The Bible will never steer me wrong.

Yours is a common point of view among Evangelical Christians who style themselves "nondenominational," but it's entirely unbiblical. There are several good reasons why you should abandon this position and give a close and prayerful look at becoming Catholic.

First, as we've seen in earlier sections of this book, the Bible nowhere says or implies that all you need is the Bible. For you to claim that you only go by those teachings you find in the Bible is simply incoherent because the Bible doesn't contain *that* teaching.

Second, Christ established a particular Church, not some amorphous "nondenominational" movement of Christians. The very notion of the kind of free-floating, Bible-only "nondenominationalsim" you espouse is alien to the Bible and to the reality of how the early Church lived (not to mention the succeeding centuries of the Church). Christ said, "On this rock I will build *my church*, and the gates of hell will not prevail against it." He did not say, "On this rock I will build a network of loosely affiliated non-denominational fellowships." If you really believe what the Bible says about the Church Christ established,[199] you should seek out that Church and become a member, for there you will find Christ in all His fullness, and His teachings in all their authenticity. Remember that Christ said He wanted "all nations" to become disciples (i.e., members) of that Church. His revelation, and that of the Holy Spirit given through the ministry of the apostles, in their preaching[200] and writing of Scripture,[201] forms a body of doctrine (the Deposit of Faith) that we are obligated to observe. "*Why do you call me 'Lord, Lord,' and not do what I tell you?*" (Luke 6:46).

And third, have you ever stopped to wonder how it is that the Bible seems to have steered wrong everyone *else* who differs with you? For example, the fact that you're non-denominational (which is really just another form of a denomination) indicates that you disagree with at least some of the teachings of the Evangelical Lutherans, Anglicans, Church of Christ,

Southern Baptists, Orthodox Presbyterians, Methodists, Reformed Baptists, and other more conservative Bible-only groups. If you agreed with and subscribed to everything the Southern Baptists teach and practice, it would logically follow that you would be a Southern Baptist. But you aren't a Southern Baptist almost certainly because there are some teachings of theirs with which you disagree. Ditto for the other groups. And there's the rub. Each of those groups claims to go by the Bible alone, as you do. Yet you claim the Bible will never lead you astray, while at the same time you are implicitly asserting that the Bible, apparently, has led all of those groups astray!

Consider, for example, the Lutheran teaching on infant baptism.[202] Lutherans believe that the Bible teaches plainly that infants can and should be baptized, and it offers biblical proof for this teaching. Yet Southern Baptists reject that teaching as "unbiblical"[203] and heretical. One Southern Baptist minister recently wrote:

> If one were to come to me from a Lutheran church, I would note that Lutherans take a sacramental view of baptism. The Lutheran apple of the Reformation didn't fall that far from the Roman Catholic tree on this issue. They teach that baptism affects faith in the recipient, even if he or she is a newborn, and that is emphatically not a Baptist understanding.

So I would ask the Lutheran to submit to our baptism. Luther's baptism is not John Smyth's[204] baptism. We are in Luther's debt for his advancing such doctrines as salvation by faith alone, trust in Scripture alone, the priesthood of believers, the sacredness of "secular" vocations, but we are not in his debt for his understanding of baptism, for it is essentially pre-Reformation.[205]

So which group did the Bible lead astray on this issue, the Baptists or the Lutherans? One of these two is wrong about the issue of infant baptism. Their positions are diametrically opposed, so there is no middle ground here. Either you will have to posit that the Bible led one group or the other astray on this central issue, in which case your "Bible only" position collapses in on itself because there would be an inarguable example of the Bible not being sufficient to correct a misunderstanding on an important issue such as baptism, or you will have to say that the Bible didn't lead the Lutherans or the Southern Baptists astray, but rather one of these groups *misinterpreted* the Bible.

But now look what happens. If one of these groups, in spite of their undoubted sincerity, prayerfulness, and best efforts, misinterpreted the Bible, then how can you be so sure that *your* interpretations of the Bible are accurate? The answer, of course, is that you can't be any more certain your interpretations of the Bible are correct than can the Baptists or Lutherans. And this demonstrates the need for an authoritative teaching Church — which happens to be the Catholic Church.

As we saw in earlier chapters, only the Catholic Church is able to demonstrate that its interpretation of the Bible is consistent with how the early Christians interpreted the Bible. The reason for this consistency is that the early Church was the Catholic Church. And it's in the Catholic Church, ever ancient, ever new, that you will encounter the complete teachings of Jesus Christ and the apostles. There you will find the authentic interpretation of the Bible. There you will find the fullness of truth. I invite you to lay aside whatever prejudices and preconceptions you may have about the Catholic Church and come home. It's where Christ wants you. It's where He's waiting for you with open arms.

BOOKS OF THE BIBLE

40. Why did the Catholic Church add the Apocrypha to the Bible at the Council of Trent, when the Bible say in Revelation 22:18-19: "I warn every one who hears the words of the prophecy of this book: if any one adds to them, God will add to him the plagues described in this book, and if any one takes away from the words of the book of this prophecy, God will take away his share in the tree of life and in the holy city, which are described in this book."

You have been misled. The Catholic Church did not add the Deuterocanonical books (or the "Apocrypha," as many Protestants pejoratively refer to them) at the Council of Trent. On April 8, 1546, in its fourth session, the Council of Trent formally declared the canon of the Old and New Testaments, giving the complete list of the canonical books. But though this was the first time in which each of the canonical books was named individually, this was by no means the first time the Catholic Church had proclaimed the canon of Scripture, which included the contested seven books of the Old Testament known as the Deuterocanonical books.[206] About one hundred years earlier, at the Council of Florence, the canon of Scripture was also formally declared.[207]

In the early Church there were also authoritative declarations of the canon, each of which included the seven Deuterocanonical books: at the Synod of Rome (A.D. 382), and the regional Councils of Hippo (A.D. 393), and Carthage (A.D. 397). About that same time, the Council of Laodicea[208] also listed the canonical books, as did Pope Innocent I in A.D. 405 in an epistle to Bishop Exuperius of Toulouse. At the Seventh Ecumenical Council, Nicea II (A.D. 787), the "African Code," as the North-African regional synods of Hippo and Carthage that proclaimed the canon of Scripture were also known, was formally proclaimed as accepted by the Council, although the specific books of the canon were not listed by name in the canons and decrees of Nicea II.

That bit of historical background helps pave the way toward a clearer understanding of the question of the Deuterocanonical books. The Catholic Church did not add them at the Council of Trent. Rather, it was the early Protestant reformer Ulrich Zwingli who most notably deleted the Deuterocanonical books from his edition of the Bible. Martin Luther also argued that they were not canonical, and though he, too, removed them from the Old Testament section of his edition of the Bible, because certain teachings in them (e.g., the existence of purgatory and the efficacy of prayers for the souls of the departed, presented in 2 Maccabees 12), clashed with his new theological system, he retained them in a separate appendix between the Old and New Testaments. Luther's rationale for deleting those canonical books was that the Hebrew Bible did not contain them, though the Septuagint (i.e., Greek) version of the Old Testament, which was the version used by the vast majority of Jews at the time of Christ and the apostles, did contain them. He argued that the Jews who compiled the Hebrew Canon[209] did not include those books would know better than anyone if they belonged.[210] He also, by the way, sought to eliminate the Letter to the Hebrews, the Letter of James, the Letter of Jude, and the Book of Revelation! Happily, his followers were able to dissuade him from such a disastrous maneuver.

Another detail of this issue that's unknown to many Christians is that, for roughly the first three centuries after the start of the Protestant Reformation, virtually all Protestant Bibles contained the Deuterocanonical books! In fact, it wasn't until 1827 that the first major Protestant edition (i.e., produced by the British and Foreign Bible Society) finally eliminated the books altogether.

Another important issue you should be aware of is that, in Revelation 22:18-19, St. John was warning specifically against tampering with the Book of Revelation, not the Bible.[211] After all, "this book" he referred to was the book he had just finished writing, not the Bible itself, since the compilation by the Catholic Church of the canonical Scriptures into a single volume or "book," as we know it today, was still centuries away. One key proof that this is so is that Moses issued a very similar warning in Deuteronomy 4:2 and 13:1 where he admonished the people not to "add to the word which I command you" from the commandments he enjoined on them by the revelation of God.[212]

Now the real question for you to ponder is this: Given that the Christian Church, from the early centuries, included these seven books in the Bible, and given that it was in reality the Protestant Reformers, not the Catholic Church, that sought to delete them from the Bible, don't you think you should re-examine your question and prayerfully consider embracing the Catholic version of Scripture, which is, in fact, the complete version? Do you *really* want to miss out on a portion of God's written Word? I sure hope not!

41. Jesus Christ said, "And call no [man] your father upon the earth: for one is your Father, which is in heaven" (Matt. 23:9, King James Version). Why do Catholics violate this teaching by calling priests "father"?

The Catholic Church is not violating Scripture by the practice of calling priests "father." The easiest way to prove that is to start with a biblical truth on which all Catholics and Protestants can heartily agree: "God is not a God of confusion but of peace" (1 Cor. 14:33). This means that it's contrary to God's nature to contradict himself. And so, if Christ had intended His comments in Matthew 23:9 about calling no man on earth "father" to be understood literally, we would expect to see that the meaning followed all other incidents where this issue comes up in Scripture. The problem with your objection to the Catholic practicing of calling priests "father" is that the biblical evidence shows conclusively that Jesus could *not* have meant literally that we shouldn't refer to humans with that term of respect.

In the opening verses of Matthew 23:2-12, just before Christ excoriates the corrupt and hypocritical Scribes and Pharisees, He says this to His apostles:

> "The scribes and the Pharisees sit on Moses' seat; so practice and observe whatever they tell you, but not what they do; for they preach, but

do not practice. They bind heavy burdens, hard to bear, and lay them on men's shoulders; but they themselves will not move them with their finger. They do all their deeds to be seen by men; for they make their phylacteries broad and their fringes long, and they love the place of honor at feasts and the best seats in the synagogues, and salutations in the market places, and being called rabbi by men. But you are not to be called rabbi, for you have one teacher, and you are all brethren. *And call no man your father on earth, for you have one Father, who is in heaven.* Neither be called masters, for you have one master, the Christ. He who is greatest among you shall be your servant; whoever exalts himself will be humbled, and whoever humbles himself will be exalted."

What does He mean by this? This is one of those passages in Scripture where it's sometimes easier to discover what Christ did not mean than what He meant. We can rule out the idea that He meant literally not to call humans beings "father," because we have so many examples of the apostles and even the Lord himself doing exactly that.

In Acts 7:2, we see the young deacon Stephen, filled with Holy Spirit, addressing the *very same men* whom Christ denounced in Matthew 23 as "brethren and fathers." Throughout his soliloquy to the Sanhedrin, Stephen repeatedly refers to various men as "father."[213]

Not only was the Holy Spirit inspiring Stephen to utter these words, but the Holy Spirit later inspired St. Luke to record them in the Book of Acts.

If Jesus Christ intended us to understand His words in Matthew 23 to mean literally "call no man . . . father," then how do you explain the fact that the Holy Spirit, the Third Person of the Blessed Trinity, in Acts 7, *violates* what Christ, the Second Person of the Trinity, said not to do? Clearly, since God is not the author of confusion, the only solution is to recognize that Jesus did not mean what you think He meant.

St. Paul echoes Stephen in Acts 22:1 when he addresses the Jewish leaders saying, "Brethren and *fathers*, hear the defense which I now make before you". Why would St. Paul do such a thing if he knew — as he most certainly would have to have known — that Christ had literally forbidden that?

Other biblical evidences to consider are Luke 16:24, where Christ refers to "Father Abraham" in His teaching about Lazarus and the rich man. In Romans 4:17-18, St. Paul also refers to Abraham as the "father of many nations." In 1 Thessalonians 2:11, he compared his ministry to the Thessalonian Christians to a "father with his children." St. John uses the same term repeatedly in his first epistle (cf. 1 John 2:13-14).

Perhaps the most compelling biblical evidence that the religious title "father" is not contrary to Christ's meaning in Matthew 23 comes from St. Paul's explanation of his own priestly ministry:

> I do not write this to make you ashamed, but to admonish you as my beloved children. For though you have countless guides in Christ, you do not have many fathers. *For I became your father in Christ Jesus through the gospel.* I urge you, then, be imitators of me. (1 Cor. 4:14-16)

Notice that not only does St. Paul call *himself* "father" in a religious sense, he urges us to imitate him!

St. Clement of Alexandria reinforced this understanding when he wrote:

> He who proclaims the truth is to be prevented from leaving behind him what is to benefit posterity. It is a good thing, I reckon, to leave good children to posterity. This is the case with children of our bodies. But words are the progeny of the soul. Hence we call those who have instructed us, fathers.[214]

And finally, here's one additional point for you and all those who argue against the Catholic practice of calling priests "father" to ponder. Remember what else the Lord said in Matthew 23: Call no one "teacher" and call no one "master." If non-Catholics who object to Catholics calling priests "father" are doctors, they are, by their own logic, violating this passage, for the word "doctor" is simply the Latin word for teacher. Similarly, if you have a master's degree, you're out of luck. Better tear up that diploma if you intend to persist in thinking Catholics are wrong for calling priests "father."

BAPTISM

42. Catholics believe in "baptismal regeneration," and that through water baptism you're born again. But that's totally unbiblical. Baptism can't save you. To be born again the Bible way means to be saved by repenting of your sins and, through faith, accepting Jesus Christ as your personal Lord and Savior.

In John 3:3-7, Jesus said one must be born by "water and spirit" and "born from above." This refers to baptism. In the preceding two chapters we see the mystical prefigurements of the Sacrament of Baptism and its effects. In chapter one, the Lord himself is baptized and we see the Holy Spirit in the form of a dove descend upon Him. In chapter two, we see the Lord perform His first public miracle at the Wedding at Cana when He transubstantiates the water contained within six stone jars that were used for "rites of purification" (cf. John 2:6). And finally, in chapter three, He gives His teaching that we are to be baptized in order to enter the kingdom of heaven. And immediately after this discourse on baptism with Nicodemus we read (cf. verse 22): "Jesus and his disciples went into the land of Judea; there he remained with them and baptized."

The Bible is clear that baptism is more than a mere symbol of our initiation into the Body of Christ. It really does what it signifies:

> Peter said to them, "Repent, and be baptized every one of you in the name of Jesus Christ *for the forgiveness of your sins; and you shall receive the gift of the Holy Spirit.*" (Acts 2:38)

It doesn't get much clearer than that.

> Do you not know that all of us who have been baptized into Christ Jesus were baptized into his death? We were buried therefore with him by baptism into death, so that as Christ was raised from the dead by the glory of the Father, we too might walk in newness of life. (Rom. 6:3-4)

Other biblical passages to consider are: Acts 22:16; 1 Cor. 6:11; Col. 2:11-14; Titus 3:3-7; and 1 Peter 3:18-21.

If the common Anabaptist theory that baptism is an ordinance that does not actually do what it signifies, then the passages above would be rendered meaningless. How can we be "baptized into" Christ's "death" and "raised" to new life by a ritual that does not do what it symbolizes? We can't. To use a parallel, when a man and a woman receive from each other the Sacrament of Matrimony, they perform a ritual that symbolizes their union in God. They join hands, exchange rings and vows, etc. Each of these elements is intended to outwardly show forth an inward reality. But remember that, by the fact that they perform this sacramental ritual, there is a *real inward change*. The two become "one flesh" (Matt. 19:6). The sacrament not only symbolizes their new union, but it also *effects* it. The same is true of the sacrament of baptism.

The teaching that baptism does regenerate the soul, cleansing it from sin, both original and actual, and infuses into it the graces and gifts of the Holy Spirit, is universal in the early Church, as these representative quotations make clear:

The Epistle of Barnabas, A.D. 170 — "Regarding [baptism], we have the evidence of Scripture that Israel would refuse to accept the washing which confers the remission of sins and would set up a substitution of their own instead" (11:1).

St. Gregory of Nazianzus — "Let us be buried with Christ by Baptism to rise with him; let us go down with him to be raised with him; and let us rise with him to be glorified with him" (*Oratio*, 40).

St. Hilary of Poitiers — "Everything that happened to Christ lets us know that, after the bath of water, the Holy Spirit swoops down upon us from high heaven and that, adopted by the Father's voice, we become sons of God" (*On Matthew*, 2, 5).

43. The Bible says nothing about baptizing infants, yet the Catholic Church practices infant baptism. Why?

As far as any explicit statement goes, the Bible is silent on whether children should be baptized or not. The implicit evidence in favor of baptizing infants and children, however, is broad and compelling.

First, recall that the New Testament Sacrament of Baptism replaced the Old Testament ordinance of circumcision.[215] In the days before Christ, circumcision was performed predominately upon infants — eight-day-old boys.[216] The ritual of circumcision was performed on a baby who could not have had even the slightest understanding of (much less desire for) the covenant his parents were making with God on his behalf. Even so, that covenant was valid in the eyes of God. So, too, when Christian parents bring their infant son or daughter to be baptized, they are covenanting with God on behalf of that child, and the regenerating grace that comes from the sacrament is infused into that child's soul in spite of his unawareness of what is happening. In the same way that a child is born into the world from the womb of his mother and has no capacity to comprehend (much less choose) what is happening to him, so, too, a child can be reborn into the life of Christ through grace and not be able to comprehend the gift of grace being bestowed on him.

Also, in Mark 2:1-12, we see another crucial piece of biblical evidence demonstrating that God will grant grace to someone because of the efforts made by a third person on his behalf.[217] This is the story of the Healing of the Paralytic. He was so enfeebled by his illness that he could not approach Christ on his own. Rather, his friends, out of an admirable desire to see him healed, went so far as to tear open the roof and lower the man down to the floor in front of Christ. The remarkable thing is that "when Jesus saw *their* faith, he said to the paralytic, 'My son, *your* sins are forgiven.' " This passage is an excellent parallel to infant baptism. The faith of the parents is pleasing to God, as is their desire to have their child baptized and receive the graces of the sacrament. They want their baby to be saved and, as St. Peter declared in 1 Peter 3:18-21, "Baptism . . . now saves you."

St. Peter touched on this issue when he said: "Repent, and be baptized every one of you in the name of Jesus Christ for the forgiveness of your sins; and you shall receive the gift of the Holy Spirit. For the promise is to you and to your children and to all that are far off, every one whom the Lord our God calls to him."[218] Not only do we see the effects of baptism (forgiveness of sins and the reception of the Holy Spirit), we see that even though Jesus begins His statement with the command "repent," He stresses that the promise of the gifts to be received in baptism are not restricted just to adult believers, but also to children. And He makes no distinctions here (or elsewhere, for that matter) about the age of the child being baptized. Some may argue that Peter's command to "repent" is a prerequisite for baptism and that if one does not have the capacity to repent he cannot be baptized, but this argument falls apart at the seams when we apply that same illogic to a passage such as 2 Thessalonians 3:10, where St. Paul says that if someone does not work, he shouldn't be allowed to eat. But infants can't work. Does this mean they should not eat? Of course not. The parallel between these two passages is helpful in understanding Peter's words in Acts 2. The "repent" command is binding on those who have the ability to repent. It is not binding (how could it be?) on those, such as infants and the mentally retarded, who don't have that ability.

Recall also that St. John the Baptist was "filled with the Holy Spirit" when he was yet still in his mother's womb. If the typical Protestant argument against infant baptism were valid, this passage would make no sense. That's because even as a fetus, the infant St. John the Baptist was able to receive this special gift of God's grace though he was entirely unable to repent — nor did he need to, since he had committed no sins.

That Christ intends for children to be baptized becomes even clearer when we examine his words in Luke 18:15-17:

> Now they were bringing even infants[219] to him that he might touch them; and when the

disciples saw it, they rebuked them. But Jesus called them to him, saying, "*Let the children come to me, and do not hinder them;* for to such belongs the kingdom of God. Truly, I say to you, whoever does not receive the kingdom of God like a child shall not enter it."

How do we come to Christ and become members of His mystical Body? Through baptism. Read these passages to verify this: John 3:3-5, 22, Mark 16:15-16, Acts 16:30-33, Acts 22:16, Romans 6:2-4, 1 Corinthians 6:11, Colossians 2:11-14, Titus 3:3-7, and Hebrew 10:21-22.

And finally, don't forget that the practice of infant baptism was universal in the early Church. The early Church Fathers[220] are unanimous and emphatic that the historic Christian teaching on infant baptism comes directly from the apostles themselves. Happily, the mistaken notion that only adult believers can be baptized was an aberration that wouldn't rear its head for quite some time.

CONFESSION OF SINS

44. Why do Catholics confess their sins to a priest? I see several problems with this. First, it's unbiblical. Second, priests are sinners just like anyone else, so how can they forgive sins? And third, 1 Timothy 2:5 says, "There is one mediator between God and man,

the man Christ Jesus." So the priest can't be a mediator between you and God to forgive your sins.

Let's answer your objections in reverse order. First, it's true that Christ is the "one mediator between God and man."[221] As God himself, only Christ could bridge the gap of sin that separated us from God. No human person could do that. It's in that unique and all-important sense that St. Paul meant that Christ is the "one mediator." But the Bible makes it clear that St. Paul did not thereby rule out the fact that human beings can participate in subordinate ways in Christ's own unique ministries.

St. Thomas Aquinas explained it this way:

> "Properly speaking, the office of a mediator is to join together and unite those between whom he mediates: for extremes are united in the mean (Latin: *media*). Now to unite men to God perfectly belongs to Christ, through Whom men are reconciled to God, according to verse 19 in 2 Cor.: "God was in Christ reconciling the world to Himself. And, consequently, *Christ* alone is the perfect Mediator of God and men, inasmuch as, by His death, He reconciled the human race to God."[222]

There are many biblical references to this principle of a subordinate participatory share in the ministry of Christ. For example, Christ suffered "once for all"[223] in a perfect and complete sacrifice to the Father for our redemption.

Even so, the Bible says that the Lord shares that redemptive mission with every Christian, each of whom is a member of the Body of Christ and has a subordinate and limited share in the mystery of the Lord's suffering. St. Paul speaks about this when he says, "Now I rejoice in my sufferings for your sake, and in my flesh I complete what is lacking in Christ's afflictions for the sake of his body, that is, the church."[224]

Christ is the supreme judge.[225] And the Bible says that Christians are also called to a share in His judgeship, as judges in heaven.[226] Similarly, the Bible says that Christ is the Good Shepherd,[227] but yet certain men are called to the office of shepherd.[228] In fact, St. Peter (the first shepherd of the Church after Christ[229]) wrote that Christ is the "chief shepherd,"[230] which indicates that there are other shepherds who share in His ministry.

Christ is the creator of the universe (John 1:1-3, Col. 1:16-17, Heb. 1:1-2), but He shares that creative role with men and women who, through sexual intercourse, become co-workers with Him in the divine plan of life. He is also the high priest of the new and eternal covenant.[231] And yet, all Christians share in His priesthood generally through baptism,[232] and some do more specifically through the Sacrament of Holy Orders.

Christ is the King of Kings,[233] yet Revelation 4:4-10 says that the blessed in heaven will share in His royal kingship.[234] Revelation 3:21 says, "He who conquers, I will grant him to sit with me on my throne, as

I myself conquered and sat down with my Father on his throne."[235]

Christ is the divine physician who heals us of our self-inflicted wounds of sin and rebellion and reconciles us to the Father, but He also shares this ministry of healing and reconciliation with those in His Church appointed to that task.[236] We can see that it fits perfectly with the Lord's plan that He would share His ministry of forgiving sins with those He appointed to that mission: the bishops, priests, and deacons.

Now for your second objection: that priests are sinners like everyone else. That's absolutely true. But remember that Christ chooses to work through sinful human beings.[237] St. Peter, St. John, St. James, St. Paul, and *all* the Apostles (indeed, *all* Christians, with the exception of the Blessed Virgin Mary) were sinners in need of God's mercy and grace. Even so, the Lord used them to forgive sins:

> Jesus said to them again, "Peace be with you. *As the Father has sent me, even so I send you.*" And when he had said this, he breathed on them, and said to them, "Receive the Holy Spirit. If you forgive the sins of any, they are forgiven; if you retain the sins of any, they are retained." (John 20:21-23)[238]

Notice that in addition to granting the apostles the power (His power) to forgive sins, it is Christ the high priest who is sent by the Father to reconcile the world, who in turn sends His apostles forth to do the same thing: reconcile all people from sin and death into the peace and life of grace. This mission He gave them is the "ministry of reconciliation" (cf. 2 Cor. 5:18-20).

> Is any among you sick? Let him call for the elders [presbyters][239] of the church, and let them pray over him, anointing him with oil in the name of the Lord; and the prayer of faith will save the sick man, and the Lord will raise him up; *and if he has committed sins, he will be forgiven.* Therefore confess your sins to one another, and pray for one another, that you may be healed. The prayer of a righteous man has great power in its effects. (James 5:14-16)

And the third part of your objection, that confessing one's sins to a priest is "unbiblical," can best be answered by showing what the Bible does, in fact, say about this. Note that in 1 John 1:9, we're told that, "If we *confess* our sins, he is faithful and just, and will forgive our sins and cleanse us from all unrighteousness." Notice that the forgiveness for sins is connected with the act of confessing those sins. A corollary to this is: If we *don't* confess our sins, we will not receive forgiveness.

The question now is to see how the Lord expects us to confess our sins. Should it be simply a private confession to God in the privacy of one's own mind, or did Christ establish an external forum for confession of our sins? The biblical evidence shows that it's not an either-or proposition — either confession directly to God *or* confession to one who was appointed by God to forgive sins — rather, Scripture is clear that it's a both-and injunction that Christ has given us.

In John 20:21-23, Christ gives His apostles authority to forgive sins. He doesn't give them the ability to read minds, so it follows that the only way they could be in a position to exercise that ministry and forgive someone's sins would be for that person to *confess* them.

Also, notice the exact parallel between the biblical doctrine of forgiving sins in the name of Christ (cf. 2 Cor. 5:18-21) and the instances in the Gospels where Christ heals the lepers. Leprosy is a hideous disease. This terrible malady literally eats away the flesh in such a way that the disfigurement is so horrendous that, in New Testament times, those who had leprosy were evicted from society. They had to live apart from the general population, usually subsisting in caves or other remote locales. The prime reason for forcing lepers to live apart, though, was not their disfigurement but the fact that they were highly contagious.

In Mark 1:40-44 we see a leper approach Christ and beg for healing:

> And a leper came to him beseeching him, and kneeling said to him, "If you will, you can make me clean." Moved with pity, he stretched out his hand and touched him, and said to him, "I will; be clean."

And immediately the leprosy left him, and he was made clean. And he sternly charged him, and sent him away at once, and said to him, "See that you say nothing to any one; but go, show yourself to the priest, and offer for your cleansing what Moses commanded, for a proof to the people."[240]

Notice the striking parallels between this episode with the Leper and the Sacrament of Confession. First, the Leper appealing directly to Christ parallels the Christian who goes to God directly in the privacy of his heart and begs forgiveness for his sins. In fact, one cannot worthily receive the Sacrament of Penance without first going directly to God and confessing one's sins with heartfelt repentance.

Second, notice that Christ heals the leper but He doesn't simply send him on his way. There is another dimension to this disease that must still be dealt with: its effects on the community. You see, the townsfolk would have had no idea that the leper had been healed. So he couldn't very well go waltzing back into town expecting to resume his previous life among the others. They would panic upon seeing him because leprosy was so contagious and they would be afraid of contracting it from him. So what does the Lord do? He commands the man to "show [himself] to the priest, and offer for your cleansing what Moses commanded, for a proof to the people." This parallels the Sacrament of Confession, in which the repentant sinner goes before the priest of the New Covenant, "shows himself" by making a complete and sincere confession of the sins he has already confessed directly to God. The priest acts in the name of Jesus Christ, and with the power of forgiveness that Christ imparted to His apostles (cf. 2 Cor. 5: 18-20; John 20:21-23) to pronounce the words of absolution, forgiving the sinner. This enables the sinner to re-enter the "community" of the Body of Christ.[241]

As St. Paul said, "If one member [of the Body] suffers, all suffer together. . . ."[242]

The Sacrament of Confession is the means Christ established for Christians to wash their robes in the "blood of the lamb" (cf. Rev. 7:14). Since all of us in some way or another fall through sin, Christ's loving and wise sacrament is there to help restore us to grace and heal the wounds we bring upon ourselves through sin.

THE EUCHARIST

45. When Jesus said, "This is my body" and "this is my blood" at the Last Supper, he was speaking figuratively, not literally. He said to "do this in remembrance of me" (Luke 22:19). He wants us to *remember* Him not, to imagine that He is literally present in the communion wafer. The Catholic Church's teaching on the so-called "real presence" is a sham and completely misunderstands the meaning of these passages.

Let's see about that. I should remind you that your "symbolic," or "memorial," view of the Eucharist is completely at odds with two thousand years of historic Christianity. The doctrine of Christ's Real Presence, Body, Blood, Soul, and Divinity, in the Holy Eucharist has been the constant teaching of the Catholic Church since the time of the Apostles.[243] How can you be so sure that your interpretation of the eucharistic Bible verses is correct and all the early Christians (many of whom lived very close to the time of the apostles and who spoke and read Greek, the language of the New Testament) were wrong? On what basis do you assert your interpretation as being correct over the way they interpreted the Bible? After all, you are living some two thousand years after the time of Christ. Doesn't it seem reasonable to you that if anyone would know what the Lord meant when He said "this is my body" and "this is my blood," the early Christians would have known? The fact is, the early Church was consistent and unanimous in its belief that Christ was truly present in the Eucharistic Sacrifice.[244]

46. I am offended by the Catholic Church's stance on communion. As a Lutheran, I am not allowed to receive communion at a Catholic service. Recently, a cousin of mine got married in the Catholic Church and our whole family, all Protestant, were excluded from receiving. That was very hurtful to us and I believe it just causes more division in the body of

Christ. Why won't the Catholic Church let me receive communion? At our church we allow anyone to approach the table of the Lord.

I'm sincerely sorry that this Catholic teaching on not allowing non-Catholics to receive Communion has offended you — it's not intended to offend, but to protect. You see, St. Paul himself warned about the grave spiritual danger involved in receiving the Eucharist when one should not. It's precisely for the reasons St. Paul gives that the Catholic Church does not allow non-Catholics,[245] or any Catholic in the state of mortal sin,[246] to receive the Eucharist:

> For as often as you eat this bread and drink the cup, you proclaim the Lord's death until he comes. Whoever, therefore, eats the bread or drinks the cup of the Lord *in an unworthy manner* will be guilty of profaning the body and blood of the Lord. *Let a man examine himself*, and so eat of the bread and drink of the cup. For any one who eats and drinks *without discerning the body* eats and drinks judgment upon himself. That is why many of you are weak and ill, and some have died. But if we judged ourselves truly, we should not be judged. But when we are judged by the Lord, we are chastened so that we may not be condemned along with the world. (1 Cor. 11:26-32)

There are two key elements to this passage that form the basis for the Catholic Church's teaching on who may not licitly receive Holy Communion.

First, "Whoever, therefore, eats the bread or drinks the cup of the Lord in an unworthy manner will be guilty of profaning the body and blood of the Lord." This harrowing statement points to the truth that, if one is in the state of serious sin, he should not receive the Lord's body and blood. To do knowingly do so would entail sacrilege. This prohibition extends to Catholics, not just non-Catholics.

And second, "Any one who eats and drinks without discerning the body eats and drinks judgment upon himself" points out the necessity for believing in the Real Presence of Christ in the Eucharist, to discern that this is really His body and blood, soul and divinity under the appearances of bread and wine.[247]

So it's clear that great care must be taken to avoid these two dangers St. Paul warns us against in this passage. His teaching is that one must "examine himself," both to make sure he's in the state of grace and with regard to his belief in what the Catholic Church teaches about the Real Presence. To fail in either area amounts to a spiritual catastrophe that St. Paul describes as "eating and drinking judgment upon himself," and the Catholic Church seeks to protect non-Catholics from that.

47. St. Paul says in 2 Corinthians 5:6 and Philippians 1:20-24 that for believers "to be absent from the body is to be present with the Lord." This precludes the Catholic notion of purgatory because at death, anyone who is born again will go straight to the presence of God.

This issue came up some years ago when I was a guest on an Evangelical radio program aired on a large Protestant station in Southern California. When we got around to discussing purgatory, the minister who was my counterpart raised the same argument you just did, and he misquoted both of those verses, as you just did. I don't think it was intentional, but it did give people the wrong impression of what those verses actually mean.[248] Here's how I responded to this on the air that day:

First, those verses do not say or imply that "to be absent from the body is to be present with the Lord." Neither passage in any way "disproves" the biblical doctrine of purgatory. 2 Corinthians 5:6 actually says:

> So we are always of good courage; we know that while we are at home in the body we are away from the Lord, for we walk by faith, not by sight. We are of good courage, *and we would rather be away from the body and at home with the Lord.*

So whether we are at home or away, we make it our aim to please him.

You see that St. Paul is expressing his desire to be with the Lord in heaven, but he doesn't say that a Christian who dies (i.e., is absent from the body) automatically goes straight to heaven. This is true also of Philippians 1:20-24, which says:

> [I]t is my eager expectation and hope that I shall not be at all ashamed, but that with full courage now as always Christ will be honored in my body, whether by life or by death. For to me to live is Christ, and to die is gain. If it is to be life in the flesh, that means fruitful labor for me. Yet which I shall choose I cannot tell. I am hard pressed between the two. *My desire is to depart and be with Christ, for that is far better.* But to remain in the flesh is more necessary on your account.

Again, there's nothing in this passage either that injures the doctrine of purgatory. At best, we see St. Paul grappling with a choice between two good things: going to heaven to be with the Lord or remaining in this life a while longer to continue his ministry in the Church. There are, as he points out, advantages to both, but as we'll see in the next question, he was hardly ruling out the existence of purgatory as a temporary purification for some who are destined for heaven.

48. Purgatory is a terribly unbiblical teaching. It's not in the Bible and, worse yet, it contradicts the glorious gospel of grace. Born-again believers have been washed in the blood of the Lamb. Jesus Christ's sacrifice on the cross was more than enough to pay the price of any sins they may have committed. Just before He died, Jesus said, "It is finished." So there's no need for your so-called purgatorial punishment.

Let's put your objection to the test and see what, in fact, the Bible (not to mention the early Christians) really says about purgatory. I think you'll see that it's not at all the unbiblical teaching you've been led to believe.

First, let's clear up one misconception. Just because a word like "purgatory" or "Trinity" doesn't appear in the pages of the Bible doesn't mean that those doctrines are unbiblical. The Trinity is an eminently biblical doctrine, though you'll nowhere find the word Trinity. The same is true for purgatory.

Second, we have no disagreement that when the Lord was about to die on the cross, His exclamation "It is finished" (Greek: *tetelestai*) meant that His perfect and unique sacrifice had been fully accomplished. We also agree that His perfect sacrifice was infinitely sufficient to satisfy God's justice and atone for the sins of humanity. That is official Catholic teaching.

Third, keep in mind that the Bible tells us of another place that is neither heaven nor hell. It's known variously as Sheol, Hades, the Netherworld, and Paradise.[249] Passages such as Luke 16:19-31 (Lazarus and the rich man) and 1 Peter 3:18-20 and 4:6 (Jesus preached to the souls of the dead who were in "prison"[250]) show that some people who were destined for heaven (e.g., Lazarus in Luke 16 and the spirits of the Old Testament heroes whom Christ rescued from the netherworld and brought to heaven in 1 Peter 3:18-20) were in a place that was a temporary state of waiting for the redemption of Christ.

Fourth, we need to make a distinction between the eternal penalty due to sin, which is eternal separation from God (a.k.a. hell), and the *temporal* effects of our sins, which include temporal punishments. These two types of punishments are very different, and this distinction is something one must have clearly in mind to correctly understand all sorts of biblical issues, such as original sin, purgatory, hell, and the Atonement.

The temporal effects of sin are best illustrated in Genesis 3:14-20, where God pronounces a series of maledictions against Adam and Eve, the serpent, and even the physical creation itself, all as a result of Adam and Eve's disobedience: the original sin. The eternal penalty of their sin — hell — was something Christ atoned for on the cross, and Adam and Eve's salvation and avoidance of that eternal penalty was due to their faith in God's promises and their subsequent obedience to His laws, but the temporal effects of their sin remained. Enmity with the rest of nature, having to work to eat, labor pains for women, sickness, and eventually death, were all part of the punishments God permitted to fall upon Adam and Eve and all of us, their descendants. So when you, a born-again Christian, receive Christ as your personal Lord and Savior, you correctly believe that He will forgive you of your sins and remit the eternal penalty they deserve. But you still are going to have to get up and go to work tomorrow, right? Your wife will still experience pain in childbirth; you may even someday be afflicted with cancer, or some other life-threatening disease. You might have a heart attack. And in the end you, like me and everyone else, will eventually suffer the greatest of the temporal punishments outlined in Genesis 3: You are going to die someday. Christ's atoning sacrifice paid for your sins, but it didn't wipe out the temporal effects, including the punishments I just mentioned, of your sins.

There are other biblical examples of this principle of temporal punishments due to sin that God does not eliminate even when we repent and are forgiven of our sins.

As an example, in 2 Sam. 12:13-14, we see the tragic case of King David. He had sinned by committing adultery and murder, and though the Lord forgave him when he repented, there were repercussions that followed which God did not alleviate. A form of restitution[251] was still owed:

> David said to Nathan, "I have sinned against the Lord." And Nathan said to David, "The Lord also has put away your sin; you shall not die. Nev-

ertheless, because by this deed you have utterly scorned the LORD, *the child that is born to you shall die.*"[252]

Now, how does all this fit into the doctrine of purgatory? Purgatory is the place, or process, or state (however you'd like to think of it), in which the fire of God's love purifies us from the temporal effects due to sin, which include any temporal punishments due to our sins. It's a place where only those who die in the state of friendship with God (i.e., the state of grace) and who are destined for heaven, may pass through. The doctrine is expressed clearly in the Old Testament book of 2 Maccabees 12, but since that Deuterocanonical book is likely not in your Protestant Bible, let's turn to St. Paul's explanation of purgatory in 1 Corinthians 3: 10-15.

According to the commission of God given to me, like a skilled master builder I laid a foundation, and another man is building upon it. Let each man take care how he builds upon it. For no other foundation can any one lay than that which is laid, which is Jesus Christ. Now if any one builds on the foundation with gold, silver, precious stones, wood, hay, stubble — each man's work will become manifest; for the Day will disclose it, because it will be revealed with fire, and the fire will test what sort of work each one has done. If the work which any man has built on the foundation survives, he will receive a reward. If any man's work is burned up, he will suffer loss, though he himself will be saved, but only as through fire.

This passage is an excellent presentation of the Catholic teaching on purgatory. The essential elements are these:

First, the person being described here died in the state of friendship with Christ. He had "built" his life on the "foundation that is Jesus Christ."

Second, the "day" on which the deeds of this person's life are disclosed takes place after his death. "[I]t is appointed for men to die once, and after that comes judgment" (Heb. 9:27). He is now standing before God giving an account of his life.

Third, some things in his life are noble, and St. Paul compares them to "gold," "silver," and "precious stones." These elements of virtue and holiness are refined and retained. But there are other, ignoble, aspects of this man's life: the things he has to be purified of. St. Paul likens them to "wood," "hay" and "straw." These flammable materials are burned away until all that remains is the noble elements. They must be removed, of course, because as the Bible makes clear: "Nothing unclean shall enter it" (Rev. 21:27). [253]

Fourth, St. Paul says this process involves suffering, and he uses the metaphorical language of passing through fire to describe the pain of this purification. It hurts, but it hurts so good because all the dross of sin that clings to the soul at the moment of death — selfishness, anger, unrepented venial sins, inordinate attachment to creatures, etc. — all of these impurities and imperfections that might be present at death are all washed away through the purifying "flames" of God's love. As the Lord himself said, "For everyone will be salted with fire" (Mark 9:49). In Isaiah 6:1-7 we see a glimpse of how a sinful man is purified by fire.

Frequently in Scripture, God's presence is expressed by fire. For example, God appears to Moses as a burning bush in Exodus 3. We see God's presence with His people as a pillar of fire (Exodus 13-14). The angels who stand closest to God's throne are the seraphim,[254] a Hebrew word that literally means "the burning ones." God the Holy Spirit descended on the apostles in the upper room in the form of tongues of fire (Acts 2). And Hebrews 12:29 says, "Our God is a consuming fire." This fire imagery tells us something important about God. The closer you get to Him, the more you will feel the effects of His fiery presence. If you are wicked, His fiery presence will burn you (cf. Rev. 20:9). If you love Him, the fire of His love will purify you.

Fifth, and finally, we see that this process of purification takes place before the man enters heaven. It's a prelude to his entrance into glory. "He *will be saved* [future tense], but only as though passing through fire." So his eternal joy in God's presence begins only after he has passed through the flames of this purification.

So you see, even though St. Paul didn't use the term "purgatory" to describe this process of purification that some, perhaps many, will undergo before entering heaven, the principle of that purification is very clear. It's a temporary process of passive purification performed by God as a way to cleans and completely wash the sinner in the blood of the Lamb. Once it's complete, the soul is ready to see God face-to-face.[255]

Hebrews 12:22-23 says that as one approaches God's presence in heaven, he encounters angels as well as the "spirits of just men made perfect." Clearly their being made perfect took place before they entered heaven, since nothing unclean or imperfect (in however minor a way) can exist in heaven before the throne of God.

As St. Augustine of Hippo taught, it is God's fiery love that purifies and perfects all who come to Him, cleansing them from whatever imperfection of sin might prevent them from total unity with Him in heaven:

> That there should be some fire even after this life is not incredible, and it can be inquired into and either be discovered or left hidden whether some of the faithful may be saved, some more slowly and some more quickly in the greater or lesser degree in which they loved the good things that perish, through a certain purgatorial fire.[256]
> (*Handbook on Faith, Hope, and Charity*, 18:69)

St. Augustine was one of the greatest, most erudite and holy of the early Church Fathers. His knowledge of Scripture and Apostolic Tradition was masterful. If someone such as he was convinced that purgatory is a biblical doctrine, shouldn't you at least give it a second thought and prayerfully reexamine the evidence that supports it?

THE RAPTURE

49. Why doesn't the Catholic Church teach about the rapture and the end-times? The Bible clearly teaches the rapture in passages such as 1 Corinthians 15:51, and especially in 1 Thessalonians 4:15-17.

The Catholic Church does indeed teach about the coming end-times[257] (also referred to as "eschatology"), but it rejects as unbiblical the "pre-tribulation rapture" theory that's wildly popular among many Fundamentalists and Evangelical Protestants.

There are several important reasons why the rapture theory won't hold water biblically. First, though, let's define it and explain how it fits into the end-times scenario made popular by the *Left Behind* series of books.

The main version of the rapture theory is the "pre-tribulation" view, which holds that "the Church" (which is a Fundamentalist and Evangelical code for "born-again believers") will be raptured out of this world immediately prior to the Great Tribulation. Adherents of the rapture theory believe this tribulation will last for seven years. During this time, the Antichrist[258] and the Great Beast[259] will arise and great calamities, persecution, and bloodshed will ensue. At the end of that tribulation period (so the theory goes), Jesus Christ will return to establish a literal one thousand-year kingdom on earth.[260] At the end of that one thousand-year reign, the world will end, He will judge the nations,[261] and then everyone will go either to heaven or hell for all eternity.[262]

One of the problems with this theory is that it would means that one thousand seven years would elapse between the secret and silent "rapture," in which Christ returns invisibly and only for Christians, and when the Lord returns on the Last Day. But in John 6:54, Christ tells us that the dead in Christ will rise "on the *last* day."[263]

Another reason to reject the rapture theory is that it is a novelty within Christian Tradition. It only became known toward the end of the 19th century, which saw the rise of feverish "end-times" sects such as the Jehovah's Witnesses, the Mormons, and the various Adventists groups, the most prominent of which are the Seventh-Day Adventists. For the eighteen hundred years of Christianity prior to the mid-19th century, the rapture theory, as it's commonly understood today, was essentially unknown.

But the biggest reason to reject the rapture theory is the biblical problem. Let's examine five of the most commonly cited verses used by adherents to the rapture theory and see whether or not the Bible really "clearly teaches" this notion of a pre-tribulation rapture.

> **I Thessalonians 4:16-17 —** For the Lord himself will descend from heaven with a cry of command, with the archangel's call, and with the sound of the trumpet of God. And the dead in Christ will rise first; then we who are alive, who are left, shall be caught up[264] together with them in the clouds to meet the Lord in the air; and so we shall always be with the Lord.

First, notice that there is nothing in this passage that would identify this event[265] as anything other than the Second Coming of Christ, nor does it in any way even hint that it will take place prior to a period of tribulation. These are two major false assumptions that believers in the rapture are simply reading into the text.

Second, Dispensationalist Protestants[266] insist that they interpret the Bible literally unless a passage is obviously symbolic. But when it comes to the rapture, that isn't what happens. In 1 Thessalonians 4, for example, the literal sense of the passage shows that the event being described here is both public and audible. It's the exact opposite of the "secret," or "hidden," view that those who promote the rapture theory have adopted. They claim Christ will come secretly and silently at the rapture, and the only ones who will know about it will be those who are raptured.

According to the popular "left behind" rapture teaching, those who are not raptured (i.e., those who weren't "born again") will not realize that the rapture took place. It won't be public or noticeable. And that makes it completely inconsistent with 1 Thessalonians 4. The notion that only those who are raptured will see and hear what St. Paul describes in that passage is another example of reading into the biblical text something that just isn't there.

> **1 Corinthians 15:51-52** — Behold, I tell you a mystery; we shall not all sleep, but we shall all be changed, in a moment, in the twinkling of an eye, at the last trumpet; for the trumpet will sound, and the dead will be raised imperishable, and we shall be changed.

As with 1 Thessalonians 4, this often-quoted passage contains no hint of an indication that the event it describes is something separate from the Second Coming of Christ, or that it takes place prior to the tribulation period described. Also, the "twinkling of an eye" refers to the physical metamorphosis of the mortal body to a glorified body,[267] not to the speed of the rapture. Also, this passage can't be referring to the rapture since it specifically ties this event to the blast of the "last trumpet," which will herald the Second Coming of Christ.[268] This is not a reference to some "secret," "silent" rapture, but rather to the Parousia, the Second Coming of Christ, as the Catholic Church has consistently interpreted this passage for the last two thousand years.

> **Revelation 3:10** — " 'Because you [i.e., the church at Philadelphia] have kept the word of my perseverance, I also will keep you from the hour of testing, that [hour] which is about to come upon the whole world, to test those who dwell upon the earth.' "

Again, there is no explicit or implicit indication in this verse that it refers to an event separate from the Second Coming of Christ. Also, though the phrase "keep you from the hour of testing" might seem to imply that the Church will be kept out of harm's way before the tribulation begins, we know from many other passages that Christ does not intend that for His Church. For example, in John 17:15, Christ says, "I do *not* pray that thou shouldst take them out of the world, but that thou shouldst keep them from the evil one"; and John 16:33, where he tells us, "In the world you have tribulation; but be of good cheer, I have overcome the world." In John 15:19, we read that Christians have been *chosen* "not of the world," but it does not follow that Christians will be *taken* out of the world prior to a time of tribulation.

A good example of this is the savage persecution inflicted on the Church by Emperor Nero.[269] As an interesting side note, it may well be that St. John's numerical identification of the Beast as "666" in Revelation 17:17 referred not to some future personage but to the crazed Emperor Nero. This number is an example of *gematria* (a Jewish system of using the numbers represented by the letters in the Hebrew alphabet as a code to indicate something else). When "Nero Caesar" is rendered into Hebrew, it comes out to 666.

The truth is, far from containing the rapture teaching, Scripture brims with passages that tell us the Church will endure tribulations, including the biggest tribulation of all (c.f. Matt. 24:21). The Church will come through all of them, purified and holier by the ordeal: cf. Romans 12:12, 2 Corinthians 4:4, 1 Thessalonians 3:4, and Revelation 1:9, 2:10, 7:14.

Matthew 24:37-42 — "As were the days of Noah, so will be the coming of the Son of man. For as in those days before the flood they were eating and drinking, marrying and giving in marriage, until the day when Noah entered the ark, and they did not know until the flood came and swept them all away, so will be the coming of the Son of man. Then two men will be in the field; one is taken and one is left. Two women will be grinding at the mill; one is taken and one is left. Watch, therefore, for you do not know on what day your Lord is coming."

Christ is referring here to the end-times, but more immediately He's foretelling the destruction of Jerusalem in A.D. 70 by the Romans. Note that He says "*this* generation" (verse 34). The Lord's description here fits perfectly with the destruction of Jerusalem. Also, we should take note of His reference to Noah. He said that this future event would "be just like the days of Noah." Open your Bible to Genesis 6 and 7 and you'll see who were the people God would "blot out": the unrighteous, those who scoffed at God and lived in unrepented sin. And you'll also see who were the ones who were left alive: the righteous, Noah and his family. This is the exact opposite of the rapture theory that dispensationalists try to fabricate out of this passage. The ones who were "left behind" in Noah's day were the ones who were saved, and those who God would "destroy . . . with the earth" by the flood were taken to judgment, not to safety.

One final point about Matthew 24 is this telling statement from Christ: "He who *endures to the end* will be saved" (Matt. 24:13). That is a clear reference to Christians who endure any and all tribulations God allows them to go through for their own purification. So, again, far from Matthew 24 teaching that the Church will be removed from harm's way, the one who endures through those crises is the one who will be saved.

Revelation 4:1-2 — After this I looked, and lo, in heaven an open door! And the first voice, which I had heard speaking to me like a trumpet, said, "Come up hither, and I will show you what must take place after this." At once I was in the Spirit; and lo, a throne stood in heaven, with one seated on the throne!

Many people presume that this passage is a clear reference to the rapture. But is it? Dispensationalists argue that in this passage John represents or symbolizes the Church. Interestingly, these same Protestants are quick to deny that St. John could represent the Church when, as he stood at the foot of the cross with Mary, Jesus said, "Woman, behold your son," and to John, "behold your mother" (John 19:26-27). But a Catholic would ask why, if they are indeed the "literalists" they purport to be when it comes to interpreting Scripture, do they suddenly select a *symbolic* interpretation here? I would submit that it's done simply in an attempt to bolster their rapture theory, even though, by suddenly imposing a symbolic interpretation on this passage, they violate their own stated principles of interpreting Scripture. Another example of how dispensationalists sometimes play fast and loose with the Bible is their attempt to equate the "trumpet" spoken of here in Revelation 4:1 with the mention of a "trumpet" in 1 Thessalonians 4:16. This is sloppy verse-quoting on their part, because while 1 Thessalonians speaks of a trumpet blast, Revelation 4 tells us that St. John heard a voice that *sounded like* a trumpet. This is an important distinction.

In this passage, we see St. John told to "come up here!" Dispensationalists argue that this is a glimpse of the Church (symbolized by John) being brought up from the earth to heaven in the rapture. But this interpretation poses yet another insoluble problem because in the Book of Revelation, *St. John moves back and forth between the earth and heaven.* In fact, he comes back to earth *after* he is told to "come up here" to stand in heaven before the throne of God.

St. John is on earth when his apocalyptic vision begins "on the Lord's day" (Rev. 1:9-11). Then he is told to "come up here" to heaven (Rev. 4:1-2). Later, in Revelation 21:10, he is carried back to earth into a "wilderness," where he sees the Whore of Babylon seated on the seven-headed, ten-horned scarlet Beast. Obviously, the wretched and iniquitous Whore of Babylon could not be in heaven — she's on earth. Then St. John's location changes yet again, this time to a "great and high mountain," where he sees the heavenly Jerusalem "coming down out of heaven" (Rev. 21:10). And finally, in Revelation 21, St. John is present when heaven and earth are finally united into a single, permanent reality.

So, if the rapture adherents were biblically consistent, which they aren't, this would mean that the Church (purportedly symbolized here by John) also goes back and forth between heaven and earth during the time of tribulation. But, of course, no believer in the rapture would ever agree to that.

But above all the other problems with the rapture theory, there stands an even more compelling reason to reject it. Carl Olson, a convert to the Catholic Church from Dispensational Protestantism, and an expert on dispensationalism, points out that, amazingly, even the major Protestant promoters of the rapture theory admit that it is not expressly taught in the Bible. And this is a crucial point, since these same purveyors of the rapture claim to follow the Reformation principle of *sola scriptura* (Latin: by Scripture alone).

> Although many Biblical references are used to support it, the pretribulational Rapture has no basis in Scripture. In fact, prominent dispensationalists admit that no clear and obvious scriptural support exists for this belief. [Tim] LaHaye[270] acknowledges this fact, ironically, at the start of a chapter titled "Who Says It's Obscure?":
>
> > One objection to the pre-Tribulation rapture is that no one passage of Scripture teaches the two aspects of His Second Coming separated by the Tribulation. *This is true.* But then, no passage teaches a post-Tribulation or mid-Tribulation rapture, either.[271]
>
> [John] Walvoord[272] makes the same admission in the first edition of *The Rapture Question*:

Neither pretribulationism nor posttribula-
tionism is an explicit teaching of Scripture.[273]

Walvoord removed the statement from later
editions of the book. At the end of the same book
Walvoord lists "Fifty Arguments for Pretrib-
ulationalism." None contains a passage from
Scripture explicitly teaching the pretribulational
rapture for the simple reason that none exists.[274]

HELL

**50. I don't believe in a literal hell. It's true that Christ
spoke about punishment after death for some, but I
don't agree with the Catholic Church's teaching that
hell is a permanent place where "the damned" go to
suffer punishment for eternity. A good God would
never be that cruel.**

I agree with you that God is all good and does not
cause evil. By His very nature as all-good, it would be
impossible for Him to be "cruel." But even so, the
Bible is clear that there is a real hell where, sadly, real
people go. The key to understanding the reality of hell
in light of God being all-good, is to see that those who
go to hell *freely choose* to go there by living a life of
rebellion against God's commandments and then dying in the state of unrepentance. After all, God loves

mankind, and a fundamental aspect of His love is that He respects human freedom — He will never force anyone to love and obey Him. So it's important to recognize that the damned in hell chose that destination through their stubborn impenitence, in spite of the fact that God continually offers us all the graces necessary to be saved. The man who chooses to be separated from God will eventually get his wish if he doesn't repent. And so, at death he moves from time into eternity, and all opportunity to change his mind ceases. He is judged on how he lived his life,[275] and the eternal consequence of unrepentance is that hell commences: eternal separation from God.

The Bible is clear about the existence of hell in passages such as Isaiah 33:11-14, 66:24, Matthew 25:41-46 (where the "sheep" are sent off into eternal fire), Mark 9:48, Luke 3:17, 2 Thessalonians 1:9, 2 Peter 2:4-10, and Revelation 14:11-12, 21:7-8.

In particular, notice that in Matthew 25:41, on the Day of Judgment of the nations, the Lord tells the "goats" (i.e., unrepentant sinners), "'Depart from me, you cursed, into *the eternal fire prepared for the devil and his angels*" (cf. verse 46). Now look at Revelation 20:7-10, where we're told that at the end of the world the devil and his angels will be thrown into a "lake of fire and brimstone," where they will be tormented "day and night for ever and ever." This warning is repeated in Revelation 20:13-15, where we're told that "if any one's name was not found written in the book of life, he was thrown into the lake of fire."

That was the bad news; now here's the good news. In spite of all that dire reality about hell, there is a way to avoid going there. Jesus Christ was incarnated and became flesh for our salvation. Through His atoning death on the cross, you and I can receive the graces God wants to give us so we can live a holy life and die in the state of friendship with God, which means we'll go to heaven and never have to worry about hell. Christ wants to save every human being from that terrible tragedy of eternal separation from Him. To do that, He established the Catholic Church as His visible Body[276] and endowed that Church with the sacraments that cleanse, feed, heal, and prepare us to be with Him in heaven forever. It's true that some, perhaps many, people will send themselves to hell, but that doesn't have to be true of you. The way to do this is to turn to Christ through faith with a sincere and repentant heart,[277] publicly profess Him to be your Lord and Savior,[278] enter into His Church through the Sacrament of Baptism,[279] and strive, by God's grace, to live a life of loving and faithful obedience to the teachings of Christ.[280]

Then, on that happy day, you will hear the Lord say to you those all-important words: "Well done, good and faithful servant; you have been faithful over a little . . . enter into the joy of your master" (Matt. 25:21).

ENDNOTES

[1] Likewise St. Jude: "I found it necessary to write appealing to you to contend for the faith which was once for all delivered to the saints" (Jude 3).

[2] *Apostolicam Actuositatem*, 2:6

[3] *Inter Mirifica*, 2:17.

[4] The root word is *apologia*.

[5] Just as we should never forget the other Holocausts against non-Jews, such as Hitler's death campaign against Catholics, Gypsies, and others, or Stalin's brutal extermination of Ukrainian Catholics in the 1940s, or Pol Pot's ruthless elimination of millions of hapless men, women, and children in Cambodia — all three horrors took place in the 20th century.

[6] Cf. Rom. 12: 3-10; 1 Cor. 12: 12-27.

[7] 1 Tim. 3:15.

[8] Cf. Matt. 25:31-46.

[9] Cf. John 14:1.

[10] John 3:5; Acts 2:37-39.

[11] Cf. John 6; 1 Cor. 11:23-29.

[12] Cf. Luke 10:16.

[13] Cf. Matt. 28:19-20.

[14] E.g., the Judaizers and Gnostics, and later the Arians and Monophysites.

[15] *Epistle to the Smyrneans*, 8.

[16] *Catechetical Lectures*, 26, 23.

[17] Cf. Matt. 18:18; 28:18-20; Luke 10:16.

[18] Cf. 1 Cor. 12:12-13.

[19] Cf. Jer. 32:32-25; Matt. 7:15-23; Matt. 10:1-4; Matt. 26:69-75; Mark 3:19; Luke 22:54-62;. John 6:70; John 18:2-4.

[20] Cf. Matt. 23:1-3.

[21] Cf. Mark 14:10; Acts 1:15-20.

[22] Cf. Mark 14:27-31, 66-72.

[23] Mark 14:27, 50-51. Alone among the apostles, St. John reemerged from hiding to be with the Lord at the foot of the cross: John 19:26-27.

[24] Cf. Luke 2:34.

[25] Cf. John 21:15-17.

[26] Cf. Acts 2.

[27] Cf. Acts 10.

[28] Acts 15.

[29] I.e., 1 and 2 Peter.

[30] Cf. Jer. 23:1-4; Acts 5:37-39; Rom. 8:28.

[31] Cf. Luke 6:47-49.

[32] Cf. Ex. 2:11-15.

[33] Cf. 2 Sam. 11:2-27.

[34] Cf. Matt. 28:20.

[35] As a demonstration of the utter lack of biblical evidence to support *sola scriptura,* see my formal, public debates with Protestant ministers on this question. None were able to furnish any coherent defense of this doctrine, nor could they point to even a single verse that teaches that the Bible is the sole, sufficient rule of faith. Cf. these tape sets: "Does the Bible Teach *sola scriptura?*" Patrick Madrid vs. James White; "Hold Fast to the Traditions You Were Taught," Patrick Madrid vs. Rev. Fred Needham; "Search the Scriptures, Patrick Madrid vs. Dr. Rowland Ward; "What Still Divides Us?" Patrick Madrid et al. vs. Michael Horton, et al. (available from Surprised by Truth, Inc., PO Box 640, Granville, OH 43023, 740-587-4881, www.surprisedbytruth.com).

[36] For a broader discussion of the nature and scope of Tradition, see Patrick Madrid, *Why Is That In Tradition?* (Huntington, IN: Our Sunday Visitor, 2002); Yves Congar, O.P., *Tradition and Traditions* (London: Burns & Oates); George H. Tavard, *Holy Writ or Holy Church: The*

Crisis of the Protestant Reformation (London: Burnes & Oates, 1959).

[37] "Does the Bible Teach *sola scriptura*?" debate on two audio tapes, Patrick Madrid vs. James White (Surprised by Truth, www.surprisedbytruth.com, 740-587-4881).

[38] "*Theopneustos*" literally means "God-breathed."

[39] 2 Tim. 1:13, New International Version.

[40] 2 Tim. 2:1,2 New International Version

[41] Cf. Luke 1:1-4; Rom. 6:16-17; 10:14, 27; Eph. 3:10, 4:11-16; 2 Thes 2:13; Heb. 13:17;

[42] Cf. 1 Cor. 11:2; 2 Thes 2:15.

[43] 2 Tim. 3:14.

[44] *Amathes*, the Greek term for "ignorant" here does not mean stupid or slow-witted. It might be better translated "those who are untrained," or "those who are untaught."

[45] Cf. Matt. 10:40, 16:18, 18:18, 28:20; Luke 10:16; John 14:25-26, 16:13; 1 Thes. 2:13; Tim. 3:15.

[46] "*Sola scriptura: A Blueprint for Anarchy*" (*Catholic Dossier*, March-April, 1996).

[47] See Gerhard Delling's article on *teleios* in Kittel's *Theological Dictionary of the New Testament*, Gerhard Friedrich, ed. (Grand Rapids: Wm. B. Eerdmans, 1972), vol. 8, 67-78, where he translates *teleios* as: "totality," "undivided," "complete," and "perfect." Delling gives the meanings of *artios* as: "right," "faultless," "normal," "meeting demands," and "proper" [ibid., vol. l, 475-476]. Of *exartizo* he says, "At 2 Tim. 3:17 [it] means to bring to a suitable state for Christian moral action."

[48] *The Westminster Confession*, 7.

[49] The tripartite unity of Scripture, Tradition, and the teaching authority of the Magisterium (cf. Vatican II, *Dei Verbum*).

[50] l Cor. 11:1.

[51] 2 Thes. 2:15.

[52] Happily, a lot of the digging has already been done for you! For a popular level, systematically arranged collection of quotes from the Church Fathers, listed according to doctrinal issue, see Patrick Madrid, *Why Is That in Tradition?* (Huntington, Ind.: Our Sunday Visitor, 2002) and William Jurgens, *The Faith of the Early Fathers* (Collegeville: The Liturgical Press, 1978), three volumes.

[53] E.g., the *Epistle to Pope Soter* by St. Dionysius Bishop of Corinth (A.D. 170): "For from the beginning it has been your custom to do good to all the brethren in various ways and to send contributions to all the churches in every city. . . . This custom your blessed Bishop Soter has not only preserved, but is augmenting, by furnishing an abundance of supplies to the saints and by urging with consoling words, as a loving father his children, the brethren who are journeying. . . . Today we have observed the Lord's holy day, in which we have read your letter. Whenever we do read it, we shall be able to profit thereby, as also we do when we read the earlier letter written to us by Clement" (quoted in Eusebius of Caesarea, *Ecclesiastical History*, 4:23:9, 11).

[54] The First Ecumenical Council of Nicea, A.D. 325.

[55] This paragraph and the following two are adapted from my article "*Sola Scripura: A Blueprint for Anarchy*," which appeared in the March-April, 1996 edition of *Catholic Dossier.*

[56] By the Catholic inventor Johan Gutenberg, circa 1400-1468.

[57] Cf. Patrick Madrid, *Pope Fiction: Answers to 30 Myths and Misconceptions About the Papacy* (San Diego: Basilica Press, 1999), 227-230.

[58] 1491-1547.

[59] Inter, 1537—1544.

[60] 1533-1603.

[61] Somehow, eleven copies of the *Wicked Bible*, as this defective version came to be known, survived the flames,

and one of them may be seen on display at the Bible Museum in Branson, Mo.

[62] The Orthodox Church in America lists the following as the fifteen "autocephalous" Orthodox Churches in the world: The Church of Constantinople, Church of Alexandria, Church of Antioch, Church of Jerusalem, Church of Russia, Church of Georgia, Church of Serbia, Church of Romania, Church of Bulgaria, Church of Cyprus, Church of Greece, Church of Albania, Church of Poland, Church of the Czech Lands and Slovakia, Orthodox Church in America. It adds to this list the four Orthodox Churches it refers to as "autonomous": the Church of Sinai, Church of Finland, Church of Japan, and Church of Ukraine.

[63] For copious examples of patristic statements from the early Church that demonstrate without room for doubt or denial that the Eastern patriarchs and bishops in early centuries of Christianity regarded the bishop of Rome as having a primacy of jurisdiction and authority, not merely a *primus inter pares* (Latin: first among equals), as so many today imagine they did, see *Pope Fiction* (San Diego: St. Basilica Press, 1999), *Why Is That In Tradition?* (Huntington, Ind.: Our Sunday Visitor, 2002), David Hess et al., *Jesus, Peter & the Keys* (Santa Barbara: Queenship, 1997), and William Jurgens, *The Faith of the Early Fathers* (Collegeville: The Liturgical Press, 1970), three volumes.

[64] Cf. Matt. 15:1-15; Mark 7:6-13.

[65] The Catholic Church is not a "denomination," as many imagine. It is distinct from "Protestantism," which is comprised of several thousand denominations, large and small, each of which differs from the others, to a greater or lesser extent, in doctrine.

[66] To be sure, there were any number of religious groups and sects that existed in the centuries immediately preceding Martin Luther, and some of them contained elements of theological error that were precursors to the

full-blown Protestant errors that arose in the 16th century, but these groups (e.g., the Catharists, Albigensians, Waldensians) were not strictly speaking "Protestant" in the sense we refer to those groups that took root at the time of the Reformation.

[67] Cf. Matt. 28:20.

[68] *Epistle to the Corinthians*, 1:1, 58:2-59:1, 63:2.

[69] Cf. St. Clement of Alexandria, *The Instructor of Children,* A.D. 202; St. Cyprian of Carthage, *On the Unity of the Catholic Church, On the Lapsed*, A.D. 250, etc.).

[70] Cf. *Why Is That in Tradition?, Pope Fiction, The Faith of the Early Fathers*, three vols. (Collegeville: The Liturgical Press); Rod Bennett, *The Four Witnesses: The Early Church in Her Own Words* (San Francisco: Ignatius Press, 2002).

[71] The English "close of the age" lacks the force of the underlying Greek phrase, "*heos tes sunteleias tou aionos,*" which literally means "until the consummation of the ages," which is an archaic way of saying "until the end of the world."

[72] Cf. Acts 2:37-39; 8:36.

[73] Cf. 1 Timothy 3:14-15; 4:11-16; 2 Thes. 3:14-15; 1 Peter 4:17; Matt. 18:15-18; Matt. 5:13-16; 10:40; Acts 9:31; 15:28-29; 1 Cor. 12:27-30; Heb. 13:7-17.

[74] Notice the singular form: "church," not "churches." Although in Scripture we encounter mention of various Christian "churches," scattered across the Mediterranean world during the New Testament era and beyond (e.g. Acts 9:31; 15:41; Rom. 16:16; 1 Thes. 2:14; Rev. 1:4, etc.), those were simply geographical locations of the One True Church.

[75] Greek: "*Kago de soi lego hoti sou ei petros kai epi taute te petra oikedomeso mou ten ekklesian kai pulai hadou ou katiskusousin autes.*"

[76] Cf. Matt. 18:15-18; Acts 9:31; 1 Cor. 12:12-13, 27-28.

[77] St. John speaks about mortal sin in 1 John 5:16-17: "If any one sees his brother committing what is not a mortal

sin, he will ask, and God will give him life for those whose sin is not mortal. There is sin which is mortal; I do not say that one is to pray for that. All wrongdoing is sin, but there is sin which is not mortal." The underlying Greek phrase here which we translate "mortal sin" is "*hamartia pros thanaton*," which literally means "sin unto death" (i.e., the death of the soul as a result of the loss of sanctifying grace).

[78] "Mortal sin is a radical possibility of human freedom, as is love itself. It results in the loss of charity and the privation of sanctifying grace, that is, of the state of grace. If it is not redeemed by repentance and God's forgiveness, it causes exclusion from Christ's kingdom and the eternal death of hell, for our freedom has the power to make choices for ever, with no turning back. However, although we can judge that an act is in itself a grave offense, we must entrust judgment of persons to the justice and mercy of God" (CCC 1861; cf. CCC 1854-1855).

[79] In a later section of this book we'll examine the ample biblical evidence that Christians can indeed lose their salvation.

[80] Cf. Matt. 7:21-23.

[81] 1 John 3:10-12.

[82] Cf. 1 John 3:21-24; 5:3.

[83] Cf. Rom. 5:1; Eph. 2:8.

[84] Cf. Matt. 25:31-46 and Matt. 28:18-20 (where Christ sends the Catholic Church into the whole world with the mandate to teach all people those things that He "commanded" us to believe); Matt. 23:18-35; Matt. 19:16-23;

[85] Cf. Matt. 18:6-9; Rom. 2:1-11.

[86] Cf. Rom. 16:26.

[87] For example, the heresy of Pelagianism, which the great fifth-century Catholic bishop and theologian St. Augustine inveighed vigorously against in his writings.

[88] Entering into the Lord's immediate presence in heaven for all eternity is often referred to as the "Beatific Vision"

(cf. Rev. 21:27), the point at which we are "saved" in the ultimate sense and see God face-to-face. "For now we see in a mirror dimly, but then [i.e., when we get to heaven] face-to-face. Now I know in part; then I shall understand fully, even as I have been fully understood" (1 Cor. 13:12). St. John says: "Beloved, we are God's children now; it does not yet appear what we shall be, but we know that when he appears we shall be like him, for we shall see him as he is" (1 John 3:2).

[89] Cf. Matt. 5:19-20, 7:21-23, 12:36, 19:16-23, 25:31-46; Mark 14:38; Acts 10:34-35; Rom. 1:5, 2:5-11; 6:16, 16:26; 1 Cor. 13:1-3; 2 Cor. 5:10; Phil. 2:12.

[90] For a detailed exposition of the biblical issues involved here, and a comparison between the Catholic and Reformed Protestant views, see James Akin, *The Salvation Controversy* (San Diego: Catholic Answers, 2002). I would also refer the reader to a formal debate on this subject that I had recently with a Calvinist minister in Melbourne, Australia, Dr. Rowland Ward. The debate tape set entitled "Search the Scriptures" includes nearly three hours of debate on the question: "What Must I Do to Be Saved?" (available from Surprised by Truth, Inc., www.surprisedbytruth.com, 800-234-1161).

[91] Justification here refers to "righteousness" (Greek: *dikaiosune*), the state of being in a right relationship with God. "Justification is at the same time the acceptance of God's righteousness through faith in Jesus Christ. Righteousness (or 'justice') here means the rectitude of divine love. With justification, faith, hope, and charity are poured into our hearts, and obedience to the divine will is granted us" (CCC 1991; cf. 1992-1993).

[92] *De gratia et libero arbitrio* 17 (quoted in CCC 2001).

[93] *De natura et gratia*, 31 (ibid.).

[94] Cf. Mark 16:16; John 3:36; 6:40; Rom. 6:4.

[95] Cf. Rom. 1:16.

[96] Cf. Rom. 1:5; 2: 13; 2 Cor. 5:10; Eph. 5:15-7.

⁹⁷ Cf. Matt. 8:21-23, 19:16-17, 22:34-38, 28: 20; Luke 6:46; Rom. 2:13; cf. CCC 2018: "Like conversion, justification has two aspects. Moved by grace, man turns toward God and away from sin, and so accepts forgiveness and righteousness from on high."

⁹⁸ Cf. Gen. 18:9-14, 21:1-2.

⁹⁹ Note that St. Paul uses the word "if" four times in this passage. The clear implication is that if we do not remain faithful to Christ, we will be lost. The Lord doesn't go back on His promises, but we can certainly go back on ours through grievous sin. And to die unrepentant in that state of rebellion against God means damnation. That is why St. Paul is warning Christians here.

¹⁰⁰ Cf. Gal. 6:2: "Bear one another's burdens, and so you will fulfill the law of Christ"; cf. Matt. 25:31-46.

¹⁰¹ Additional passages that show a believer/Christian can lose his salvation are: Ex. 32:32-33 (cf. Rom. 9:3); Ezek. 3:20-21; Matt. 24:13; Rom. 5:2, 8:25, 1 Cor. 9:27; Phil. 2:12; Rev. 22:19.

¹⁰² Cf. Matt. 25:24-40; Rom. 2:6–7, Gal. 6:6–10.

¹⁰³ Cf. Eph. 2:8-9.

¹⁰⁴ Cf. Rom. 2:6-7, Rev. 20:13.

¹⁰⁵ Cf. John 15:5–6, Rom. 11:22–23, 1 Cor. 6:9-10, 15:1–2; Gal. 5:19–21.

¹⁰⁶ Cf. Rom. 11:22–23; Matt. 18:21–35, 1 Cor. 10:11-12, 15:1–2, 2 Peter 2:20–21;

¹⁰⁷ Cf. Matt. 10:2-5; Mark 3:16-19; Luke 6:14-17; Acts 1:13.

¹⁰⁸ Cf. Acts 2:14.

¹⁰⁹ Greek: the singular forms for "you" and "your" used in this passage are *sou* and *su*; and the plural forms for "you" (i.e., "all of you") are *humas* and *hos*.

¹¹⁰ For more discussion of the New Testament and patristic evidence of the early Christian belief in Peter's primacy, see *Pope Fiction* and *Why Is that In Tradition?*

[111] Inter A.D. 344/354 — A.D. 407.

[112] For examples of such quotes, see James Likoudis, *The Divine Primacy of the Bishop of Rome and Modern Eastern Orthodoxy* (2002), available from www.credobuffalo.com.

[113] *Homily 54 on Matthew*, 3.

[114] A.D. 540-604.

[115] John IV (A.D. 582-595).

[116] Greek: *Ho'ikoumenikòs patriárches*, Latin: *Patriarcha universalis*.

[117] Adrian Fortescue, "John the Faster," *The Catholic Encyclopedia* (New York: Robert Appleton Company, 1910), volume VIII, 493-495.

[118] Died 1059.

[119] Cf. Horace K. Mann, *The Lives of the Popes* (St. Louis: Herder, 1910), vol. VI, 139-148.

[120] *Pope Fiction*, 153.

[121] Adapted from ibid., 153-156.

[122] *Epistle 68*.

[123] I.e., to the Pope, the bishop of Rome.

[124] The Pope here emphasizes the equality of all bishops, including himself, without thereby repudiating his unique authority among the college of bishops.

[125] One important predecessor on the Chair of Peter was the saintly Pope Leo the Great (reigned A.D. 440-461). A full one hundred years before the reign of Pope Gregory the Great, Pope Leo wrote (*Sermon 4*): "Yet out of the whole world, Peter alone is chosen to preside over the calling of all the Gentiles, and over all the Apostles, and the collected Fathers of the Church; so that though there be among the people of God many priests and many shepherds, yet Peter rules all by immediate commissions, whom Christ also rules by sovereign power. . . . Wherefore it is said to most blessed Peter, 'I will give to you the keys of the kingdom of heaven. Whatsoever thou shall bind on earth will be bound in heaven, and whatsoever thou shall loose on earth shall be loosed

in heaven.' The privilege of this power did indeed pass on to the other Apostles, and the order of this decree spread out to all the rulers of the Church, but not without purpose what is intended for all is put into the hands of one. For therefore is this entrusted to Peter singularly, because all the rulers of the Church [i.e., bishops] are invested with the figure of Peter. The privilege, therefore, of Peter remains, wheresoever judgment is passed according to his equity. . . . Since then, beloved, we see such a protection divinely granted to us, reasonably and justly do we rejoice in the merits and dignity of our chief, rendering thanks to the eternal King, our Redeemer, the Lord Jesus Christ, for having given so great a power to him whom he made the chief of the whole Church, that if anything, even in our time, by us be rightly done and rightly ordered, it is to be ascribed to his working, to his guidance, unto whom it was said, 'And thou, when thou art converted, confirm they brethren'; and to whom the Lord, after His Resurrection, in answer to the triple profession of eternal love, thrice said with mystical intent: 'Feed my sheep.' And this, beyond a doubt, the pious shepherd does follow even now, and fulfills the charge of his Lord, confirming us with his exhortations and not ceasing to pray for us that we may be overcome by no temptation."

[126] *Epistle 111.* "Our predecessor" here refers to an earlier pope.

[127] "My inferiors," i.e., in the order of rank, not in the order of holiness of human dignity.

[128] *Epistle XII.*

[129] 1431-1503.

[130] The author of the *Divine Comedy*, Dante Alighieri (1265-1321), pilloried several popes for their presumed wickedness by including them in his cast of characters who appear, enduring horrible punishments for their sins, deep in the pits of hell.

[131] First Vatican Council, session 4, section 9 (July 18, 1870).

[132] Cf. Matt. 16:18-19; Luke 22:31-32; 24:33-35; John 21:15-19.

[133] Cf. Matt. 16:18-19, 18:18, Luke 10:16, 22:31-32; John 21:15-17.

[134] 2 Cor. 12:9.

[135] Eph. 3:20 (Douay Rheims)

[136] Cf. John 1:18, in which the Greek term "*monogenes*" (only-born) is used.

[137] "Filioque," *The Catholic Encyclopedia* [New York: Robert Appleton Company, 1909], volume VI, 73-74.

[138] Ludwig Ott, *Fundamentals of Catholic Dogma* (Rockford: TAN Books, 1960), 63.

[139] "[T]he 'mission' or 'sending' of one Divine Person by another does not mean merely that the Person said to be sent assumes a particular character, at the suggestion of Himself in the character of Sender, as the Sabellians maintained; nor does it imply any inferiority in the Person sent, as the Arians taught; but it denotes, according to the teaching of the weightier theologians and Fathers, the Procession of the Person sent from the Person Who sends. Sacred Scripture never presents the Father as being sent by the Son, nor the Son as being sent by the Holy Ghost (emphasis added). The very idea of the term 'mission' implies that the person sent goes forth for a certain purpose by the power of the sender, a power exerted on the person sent by way of a physical impulse, or of a command, or of prayer, or finally of production; now, Procession, the analogy of production, is the only manner admissible in God. It follows that the inspired writers present the Holy Ghost as proceeding from the Son, since they present Him as sent by the Son. Finally, St. John (16:13-15) gives the words of Christ: 'What things soever he [the Spirit] shall hear, he shall speak; . . .he shall receive of mine, and show it to you. All things whatsoever

the Father hath, are mine.' Here a double consideration is in place. First, the Son has all things that the Father hath, so that He must resemble the Father in being the Principle from which the Holy Ghost proceeds. Secondly, the Holy Ghost shall receive 'of mine' according to the words of the Son; but Procession is the only conceivable way of receiving which does not imply dependence or inferiority. In other words, the Holy Ghost proceeds from the Son" (ibid. 73).

[140] E.g., Psalm 2:7; John 6:29, 8:42, 10:36, 17:3; Acts 3:26; 1 John 4:10.

[141] John 14:26.

[142] We see here a single sentence, the two-part explicit statement that the Spirit proceeds (is sent) from the Son *and* from the Father.

[143] Emphasis added.

[144] John Allen, "The Word From Rome," *National Catholic Reporter*, May 23, 2003.

[145] I.e., the official list of the twenty-seven books that comprise the New Testament, from Matthew to Revelation, as it appears in both Catholic and Protestant Bibles.

[146] Cf. 2 Tim. 3:16.

[147] Cf. Luke 1:1-4; Luke 10:16; Matthew 16:18-19; Matt. 18:18; Matt. 28:18-20, etc.

[148] *The Westminster Confession of Faith* (1646).

[149] Cf. Matt. 16:18-19, 18:18; Luke 10:16, guided by the Holy Spirit (John 14:25-26; 16:13).

[150] Patrick Madrid, "*Sola scriptura: A Blueprint for Anarchy*" (*Catholic Dossier*).

[151] For a detailed discussion of this issue, see *Why Is That In Tradition?*, 132-146.

[152] Cf. John 3:14, where Christ refers to this mysterious episode and identifies it as a type (i.e., an Old Testament foreshadowing) of His own crucifixion.

[153] Who is also known as St. John Damascene (A.D. 645-749). He reminded us that Christ himself is the

"image of the invisible God" (Col. 1:15). The Greek word for "image" there is *eikon*, from which we derive the English word "icon." If Christ himself comes to us as an "image" of God so as to enable us to better understand Him, St. John Damascene argued, it is certainly true that our sacred images are not offensive to God if they are used for the same purpose: to help us remember and love more deeply the Lord and our departed brothers and sisters, the saints in heaven.

[154] *Apologetics Sermons Against Those Who Reject Sacred Images*, 2:5, circa A.D. 725.

[155] Cf. Matt. 12:47-50, 13:55-56; Mark 3:31, 6:3; Luke 8:19; John 2:12, 7:3-5; Acts 1:14; 1 Cor. 9:5.

[156] Cf. Matt. 1:2-11; Acts 7:23; Gal. 1:19.

[157] Cf. Matt. 23:8.

[158] Cf. Matt. 25:40.

[159] Cf. Acts 3:17.

[160] Cf. Matt. 5:47.

[161] Matt. 23:8; Rev. 22:9.

[162] Also rendered as "Judas."

[163] The bishop of Jerusalem (cf. Acts 12:17, 15:13, 21:18; Gal. 1:19; 2:9-12), also called "James the Less" (cf. Mark 15:40). Not to be confused with James, the brother of John, son of Zebedee (cf. John 1:35-42; Mark 3:17).

[164] Cf. Matt. 10:3, 27:56; Mark 3:18; Luke 6:15; Acts 1:13.

[165] Isaiah 55:8-9.

[166] Cf. Matt. 19:11-12; 1 Cor. 7:25-40; Rev. 14:1-5.

[167] *On Holy Virginity*, 4.

[168] Douay-Rheims translation. I selected this version because the literal meaning of the exchange between the Angel and Mary is more fully brought out. In particular, I believe that the meaning of the Angel's salutation to Mary (Greek: "*Kaire, kecharitomene*"; Latin: "*Ave, gratia plena*") is most accurately rendered in English as "Hail,

full of grace," as opposed to the more periphrastic and less accurate "Hail, O favored One" (RSV), or "Hail, favored one" (NAB).

[169] *That Jesus Christ was Born a Jew, Luther's Works* (Philadelphia: Fortress Press, 1955), vol. 45, 206.

[170] *Sermons on the Gospel of John*, 1-4.

[171] *Christmas Sermon*, 1531.

[172] *Sermons on John*, Ibid., vol. 22, 23.

[173] Ibid., vol. 22, 214-15.

[174] Ibid. vol. 45, 199.

[175] Cited in the *Corpus Reformatorum*, vol. 45, p. 348.

[176] *Sermon on Matthew*.

[177] Cited in the *Corpus Reformatorum*, vol. 1, p. 424.

[178] Cf. Dan. 3: 57-88; Rev. 4:8-11.

[179] "Then I fell down at his feet to worship him, but he said to me, 'You must not do that! I am a fellow servant with you and your brethren who hold the testimony of Jesus. Worship God.'"

[180] The religious context of Nathan's veneration of the King here is unmistakable.

[181] The King James Version renders this passage: "And David said to all the congregation, Now bless the LORD your God. And all the congregation blessed the LORD God of their fathers, and bowed down their heads, and worshiped the LORD and the king." This is yet another example of how the same act can be performed but with two different intentions.

[182] Additional biblical examples of bowing down, etc., are found in Gen. 23:7, 12; 33:3, 6, 7; 37:10; 42:5, 43:26-29, 48:9, 50:18; Num. 22:31; 1 Sam. 20:41; 2 Sam. 9:6; 14:22; 2 Kings 4:27; Is 49:23; Est. 3:2, 5; 6:13.

[183] Cf. 1 Tim. 6:15; Rev. 17:14, 19:16.

[184] The original Latin text, which includes the repetitions of each line as if a hymn that was sung, reads: "*Sub tuum praesidium, confugimus, confugimus, Sancta Dei Gen-*

itrix, Sancta Dei Genitrix. Nostras deprecations, ne despicias, ne despicias in necessitatibus nostris, Sed a periculis cunctis libera nos semper, Virgo gloriosa et benedicta. Sub tuum praesidium confugimus, confugimus, Sancta Dei Cenitrix, Sancta Dei Genitrix."

[185] *The Fear at the End of Life.*

[186] *Commentary on Mark.*

[187] *The Divine Liturgy of St. Basil.*

[188] Cf. Matt. 22:30 and Luke 20:35-36, where Christ says the saints in heaven become "like angels," not in that they change nature, from human to angel (they do not), but rather that they receive powers and abilities similar to those possessed by the angels.

[189] Cf. John 20:19; 1 Cor. 2:9; 1 Cor. 15:42-43; Phil. 3:20-21; 1 John 3:2.

[190] Cf. Heb. 12:23.

[191] Cf. 1 Cor. 15:42-43.

[192] *In 2 Sent.*, 1:2:2:1.

[193] Cf. John 8:44, 12:31; 14:30, Col. 1:13, 2:15, Heb. 2:14; 2 Peter 2:4; Jude 6; 1 John 3:8.

[194] Cf. 1 Tim. 2:1-5.

[195] Cf. John 1:1, 14.

[196] Cf. 1 Cor.13:8-13 (when "the perfect comes," i.e., when we enter into heaven, we shall "see" better and more clearly what is happening around us, including what transpires on earth.

[197] When Christ spoke these words, Abraham, Isaac, and Jacob had been physically "dead" for centuries, yet we know they are alive in heaven. Ditto for Moses, Elijah, and the other prophets.

[198] Cf. Heb. 11:39.

[199] Cf. Matt. 16:18, Matt. 28:19-20, Luke 10:16, etc.

[200] Cf. 1 Thes. 2:13.

[201] Cf. 1 John 2:1.

202 The Lutheran Church Missouri Synod adheres to the Lutheran *Augsburg Confession*, which states: "Of Baptism they teach that it is necessary to salvation, and that through Baptism is offered the grace of God, and that children [including infants] are to be baptized who, being offered to God through Baptism are received into God's grace. They condemn the Anabaptists, who reject the baptism of children, and say that children are saved without Baptism" (Article 9).

203 "Christian baptism is the immersion of a *believer* [i.e., an adult, not a child] in water in the name of the Father, the Son, and the Holy Spirit. It is an act of obedience symbolizing the believer's faith in a crucified, buried, and risen Savior, the believer's death to sin, the burial of the old life, and the resurrection to walk in newness of life in Christ Jesus. It is a testimony to his faith in the final resurrection of the dead. Being a church ordinance, it is prerequisite to the privileges of church membership and to the Lord's Supper" (*Baptist Faith and Message*, Article 8 [viewable at www.sbc.net]).

204 I.e., an early pioneer of the Anabaptist movement within Protestantism (died 1612). Smyth's *Short Confession of Faith* states: "[B]aptism is the external sign of the remission of sins, of dying and of being made alive, and therefore does not belong to infants" (Article 14).

205 Rev. Mark Coppenger, "What Should a Baptist Make of Other Baptisms?" in *First Person*, March 14, 2001, posted on the Southern Baptist Convention's website: www.sbc.net.

206 I.e., Judith, Tobit, Ecclesiasticus, Baruch, Wisdom, and 1 and 2 Maccabees, as well as the latter portions of Esther and Daniel.

207 Session 11, *Bull of Union with the Copts*, February 4, 1442.

[208] Cf. Canon 60. The authenticity of this canon has been disputed by some.

[209] At the "Council of Jamnia," circa A.D., 90-91.

[210] Problematically for Luther, the rabbis at the Council of Jamnia no longer held any authority to make such decisions, as that authority had passed out of the hands of the Jewish elders and into the hands of the apostles and their successors. Furthermore, the rabbis didn't include those seven books, not because of any doctrinal disagreements with what the books contained (far from it), but because they were unable to imagine the possibility that God could inspire Sacred Scripture in a pagan language such as Greek instead of in Hebrew. And the earliest editions of those books they could find at that time were written in Greek or Aramaic (later discoveries, such as the Qumran scrolls, discovered in 1947, have furnished evidence of earlier editions in Hebrew).

[211] Which is not to imply that one should tamper with the Bible at all!

[212] I.e., not just the Ten Commandments (cf. Exodus 20), but all the various commands God delivered to the people through Moses, as recorded in Leviticus and Deuteronomy.

[213] Cf. Acts 7:4, 8, 14, 20, 29, 32, etc.

[214] *Miscellanies*, I:1, circa A.D. 202.

[215] Cf. Col. 2:11-12.

[216] Cf. Gen. 17:11, Ex. 13:13-14; Lev. 12:2-3; Luke 1:59.

[217] Cf. Gen. 18:16-33; Matt. 8:5-13; 15:21-28; 19:13-15; Luke 7:1-20;

[218] Acts 2:38-39.

[219] The Greek word here for infant is *brephe* (root: *brephos*), which means "infant," "fetus," and "baby." It is clear that these babies could not approach Christ on their own volition, but the Lord was pleased that their parents brought them to Him.

[220] E.g., St. Irenaeus of Lyons, *Against Heresies*, 2:22; St. Hippolytus of Rome, *The Apostolic Tradition*, 21; St. Augustine, *On Baptism, On the Baptism of Infants*.

[221] Cf. 1 Tim. 2:5.

[222] *Summa Theologiae*, III, Q. 26, ad. 1.; cf. III, Q. 1, 2 ad. 2; cf. St. Augustine of Hippo, *Enarrationes in Psalmos*, 95:5.

[223] Cf. Heb. 7:27, 9:11-14, 27-28, 10:10-15.

[224] Cf. Col. 1:24-29.

[225] Cf. John 5:27, 9:39; Rom. 14:10; 2 Cor. 5:10; 2 Tim 4:1

[226] Cf. Matt. 19:28; Luke 22:30; 1 Cor. 6:2-3; Rev. 20:4.

[227] Cf. John 10:11-16.

[228] Cf. John 21:15-17; Eph. 4:11.

[229] Cf. John 21:15-17.

[230] Cf. 1 Pet. 5:4.

[231] Cf. Heb. 3:1, 4:14-15, 5:5-10, 7:15-26, 8:1, 9:11.

[232] Cf. 1 Pet. 2:4-5, 5-9; Rev. 1:6, 5:10, 20:6.

[233] Cf. Mark 15:32; 1 Tim. 1:17, 6:15; Rev. 15:3,17:14, 19:16.

[234] Cf. 1 Sam. 2:8; Luke 22:28-30; 2 Tim. 2:12; Rev. 1:6, 5:10.

[235] Cf. Matt. 19:28.

[236] Cf. Matt. 9:5-8, 18:18; John 20:21-22; Acts 2:38; 2 Cor. 5:18-20; James 5:14-15.

[237] Cf. 2 Cor. 5:18-20.

[238] Matt. 16:19, 18:18; 1 John 1:9.

[239] I.e., the "priests" of the Church.

[240] Cf. Matt. 8:4; Luke 5:14.

[241] Cf. Rom. 12: 1-5.

[242] 1 Cor. 12:12-26.

[243] For a myriad of examples of the doctrine of the Real Presence of Christ in the Eucharist drawn from the writings of the early Church, see James T. O'Connor, *The Hid-*

den Manna (San Francisco: Ignatius Press, 1988), William Jurgens, *The Faith of the Early Fathers* (Collegeville: The Liturgical Press, 1978), three volumes, Patrick Madrid, *Why Is That In Tradition?* (Huntington, Ind.: Our Sunday Visitor, 2002), and Louis Bouyer, *Eucharist* (South Bend: University of Notre Dame Press, 1968).

[244] The eucharistic sacrifice was prophesied by the prophet Malachi in Malachi 1:11.

[245] Except in certain, rare instances, as defined by canon law (cf. canon 844 §4).

[246] Canon 915: "Those upon whom the penalty of excommunication or interdict has been imposed or declared, and others who obstinately persist in manifest grave sin, are not to be admitted to holy communion." Canon 916: "Anyone who is conscious of grave sin may not celebrate Mass or receive the Body of the Lord without previously having been to sacramental confession, unless there is a grave reason and there is no opportunity to confess; in this case the person is to remember the obligation to make an act of perfect contrition, which includes the resolve to go to confession as soon as possible."

[247] Cf. *Catechism of the Catholic Church*, 1378.

[248] Unfortunately, it's not uncommon for some Protestant preachers and apologists to misquote these passages in their attempt to deny the biblical doctrine of purgatory. Worse yet, sometimes the inaccurate quoting seems to be intentional and deceitful. To give two prominent examples, see Loraine Boettner, *Roman Catholicism* (Phillipsburg: Presbyterian and Reformed Publishing Company, 1962, 5th ed.), 226; and James G. McCarthy, *The Gospel According to Rome* (Eugene: Harvest House, 1995), 120.

[249] Scripture portrays Hades (the Greek term for the Hebrew word *sheol*) as having two compartments or sections: one where the blessed repose in tranquillity, waiting for the Christ their savior to bring them to heaven (e.g.,

Abraham in Luke 16), and another, where the wicked are punished in advance of the general judgment, after which they are consigned to hell for eternity (cf. Matt. 25:31-46; Rev. 20:12-15).

250 Cf. Eph. 4:8-10.

251 "In virtue of commutative justice, reparation for injustice committed requires the restitution of stolen goods to their owner: Jesus blesses Zacchaeus for his pledge: 'If I have defrauded anyone of anything, I restore it fourfold' (Luke 9:8) directly or indirectly, have taken possession of the goods of another, are obliged to make restitution of them, or to return the equivalent in kind or in money, if the goods have disappeared, as well as the profit or advantages their owner would have legitimately obtained from them. Likewise, all who in some manner have taken part in a theft or who have knowingly benefited from it — for example, those who ordered it, assisted in it, or received the stolen goods — are obliged to make restitution in proportion to their responsibility and to their share of what was stolen" (*Catechism of the Catholic Church*, 2412; cf. 2302).

252 Cf. Dan. 4:24.

253 Matt. 22:9-13 provides another glimpse into the necessity of being prepared to enter into God's presence in heaven, the wedding feast of the Lamb. A guest arrived who wasn't dressed for the occasion. " 'Go therefore to the thoroughfares, and invite to the marriage feast as many as you find.' And those servants went out into the streets and gathered all whom they found, both bad and good; so the wedding hall was filled with guests. *But when the king came in to look at the guests, he saw there a man who had no wedding garment; and he said to him, 'Friend, how did you get in here without a wedding garment?'* And he was speechless. Then the king said to the attendants, 'Bind him hand and foot, and cast him into the outer darkness; there men will weep and gnash their teeth.' "

[254] Cf. Is 6:2-6.

[255] Cf. Matt. 5:18-30, 12:32; Rev. 7:13-14.

[256] St. Augustine of Hippo, A.D. 421, *Handbook on Faith, Hope, and Charity*, 18:69.

[257] Cf. *Catechism of the Catholic Church*, 675-677.

[258] Cf. Matt. 24:12; Luke 18:8; 1 Thes. 5:2-3; 2 Thes. 2:4-12; 1 John 2:18-22; 2 John 7. The Catholic Church teaches that this coming era will include the rise of the Antichrist and a severe persecution of Christ's followers; cf. *Catechism of the Catholic Church*, 675-677.

[259] Cf. Rev., chapters 13-17.

[260] Cf. Rev. 1-10. The Catholic Church (as well as Orthodox Churches and many Protestant groups) reject this view of a literal one thousand-year reign of Christ on the earth. Cf. *Catechism of the Catholic Church*, 865, 1186.

[261] Cf. Matt. 16:27, 25:31-46.

[262] Cf. Rev. 20:7-15.

[263] I.e., The Day of Judgment.

[264] The Greek word for "shall be caught up" is *harpagesometha* (from the root *harpazo*), which St. Jerome translated into Latin as *rapiemur* (from the root *rapere*).

[265] Which Catholics and others refer to as the *Parousia*, or Second Coming of Christ.

[266] Dispensationalism is a school of thought within Protestantism that believes salvation history is divided into various dispensations, or epochs (sometimes called "stewardships" or "administrations"), within which God dealt with mankind in particular ways and for particular reasons. He does so "progressively," in that each subsequent dispensation builds upon earlier ones. The typical breakdown of dispensations (although there is some disagreement over this among dispensationalists) is: "Innocence" (from the creation of Adam to the Fall, "Conscience" (from the Fall to the Flood), "Government" (from Noah to Abraham), "Promise" (from Abraham to Moses), "Law" (from Moses

to the death of Christ), "Grace" (from the Resurrection of Christ to the advent of the literal one thousand-year reign of Christ ["the Millennial Kingdom"]), "Millennial Kingdom" (from the inauguration of one thousand-year reign of Christ until the End of the World).

[267] Cf. 1 Cor. 15:23: "For this perishable must put on the imperishable, and this mortal must put on immortality."

[268] Cf. Matt. 24:30-31.

[269] Reigned A.D. 54-68; Cf. Eusebius of Caesarea, *Ecclesiastical History*, 3:17-19.

[270] Fundamentalist minister and co-author of the popular *Left Behind* series of books.

[271] Tim LaHaye, *Rapture under Attack: Will Christians Escape the Rapture?* (Sisters, Ore: Multnomah Publishers, 1998), 75. Emphasis added.

[272] Dispensationalist Protestant author, 1910-2002.

[273] (Findlay, Ohio: Dunham Publishing Company, 1957).

[274] Carl E. Olson, *Will Catholics Be Left Behind?* (San Francisco: Ignatius Press, 2003), 290-291.

[275] Cf. Heb. 9:27; Matt. 25:31-45; Rom. 2:1-11.

[276] Cf. Rom. 12; 1 Cor. 12.

[277] Cf. Eph. 2:8-9.

[278] Cf. Rom. 10:9.

[279] Cf. Matt. 28:18-20; Mark 16:116; John 3:1-22; Acts 2:37-41; Titus 3:5; Heb. 10:22; 1 Peter 3:21.

[280] Cf. Matt. 7:21-23; 19:16-17, 25:34-36; Luke 6:27-36, 46; Acts 10:34-35; Rom. 1:5; 2:6-7; Gal. 5:4-6; Col. 3:23; Phil. 2:12-13; James 2:14-26; 1 John 3:19-24, 5:3.

RECOMMENDED READING

A Guide to the Bible, Antonio Fuentes, Scepter Publications, 1987.

Where We Got the Bible, Most Rev. Henry G. Graham, Catholic Answers, 1997.

A Handbook of Christian Apologetics, Ronald Tacelli, S.J., and Peter Kreeft, InterVarsity Press, 1997.

An Essay on the Development of Christian Doctrine, the Venerable Cardinal John Henry Newman, University of Notre Dame Press, 1989 ed.

Hail, Holy Queen: The Mother of God in the Word of God, Scott Hahn, Doubleday, 2001.

Faith and Reason: Why Christianity Makes Sense, Austin Schmidt, S.J., and Joseph Perkins, A.M., Sophia Institute Press, 2002.

The Salvation Controversy, James Akin, Catholic Answers, 2001.

Any Friend of God's Is a Friend of Mine: A Biblical and Historical Explanation of the Catholic Doctrine of the Communion of Saints, Patrick Madrid, St. Basilica Press, 1996.

Theology for Beginners, Frank J. Sheed, Servant Press, 1982 ed.

Theology and Sanity, Frank J. Sheed, Ignatius Press, 1993.

Tradition and Traditions, Cardinal Yves M.J. Congar, O.P., Burns and Oates, Ltd., 1966.

Will Catholics Be Left Behind?: A Catholic Critique of the Rapture and Today's Prophecy Preachers, Carl E. Olson, Ignatius Press, 2003.

The Rapture Trap, Paul Thigpen, Ascension Press, 2002.

Catholicism and Fundamentalism: The Attack on "Romanism" by "Bible Christians," Karl Keating, Ignatius Press, 1988.

Where Is That In the Bible?, Patrick Madrid, Our Sunday Visitor Publishing Co., 2001.

Why Is That In Tradition?, Patrick Madrid, Our Sunday Visitor Publishing Co., 2002.

The Faith of the Early Fathers, William Jurgens, ed., three volumes, The Liturgical Press, 1979.

Pope Fiction: Answers to 30 Myths and Misconceptions About the Papacy, Patrick Madrid, St. Basilica Press, 2000.

The Four Witnesses: The Early Church In Her Own Words, Rod Bennett, Ignatius Press, 2002.

Surprised by Truth: Converts Give the Biblical and Historical Reasons for Becoming Catholic, three volumes, Patrick Madrid, Sophia Institute Press, 2000, Basilica Press.

One, Holy, Catholic, and Apostolic, Kenneth Whitehead, Ignatius Press, 2000.

The Fathers of the Church: An Introduction to the First Christian Teachers, Mike Aquilina, Our Sunday Visitor Publishing Co., 2000.

The Mass of the Early Christians, Mike Aquilina, Our Sunday Visitor Publishing Co., 2001.

The How-To Book of the Mass, Michael Dubruiel, Our Sunday Visitor Publishing Co., 2002.

The Shepherd and the Rock: Origins, Development, and Mission of the Papacy, J. Michael Miller, *C.S.B.,* Our Sunday Visitor Publishing Co., 1999.

Encyclopedia of Catholic Doctrine, Russell Shaw, ed., Our Sunday Visitor Publishing Co., 2001.

The Hidden Manna, James T. O'Connor, Ignatius Press, 1986.

The Lamb's Supper: The Mass as Heaven on Earth, Scott Hahn, Doubleday, 1999.

The Russian Church and the Papacy, Vladimir Soloviev, Catholic Answers, 2003.

Fundamentals of Catholic Dogma, Ludwig Ott, TAN Books, 1966 ed.

A History of Christendom, Warren Carroll, four volumes, Christendom College Press, 1985-2000.

The Christian Faith: In the Doctrinal Documents of the Catholic Church, J. Neuner, S.J., and J. Dupuis, S.J., eds., Alba House, 1996.

Mary: A History of Doctrine and Devotion, Hilda Graef, Sheed & Ward, London, 1999.

Mary and the Fathers of the Church: The Blessed Virgin Mary in Patristic Thought, Luigi S.M. Gambero, Ignatius Press, 1999.

Search and Rescue: How to Bring Your Family and Friends Into — or Back Into — the Catholic Church, Patrick Madrid, Sophia Institute Press, 2001.

Rapture: The End-Times Error That Leaves the Bible Behind, David Currie, Sophia Institute Press, 2003.

Upon This Rock, Steve Ray, Ignatius Press, 1998.

Envoy magazine, the award-winning journal of Catholic apologetics and evangelization edited by Patrick Madrid, contains hundreds of articles and departments on doctrine, Scripture, the early Church Fathers, and apologetics. To subscribe, call 800-55-ENVOY, or visit *Envoy* magazine's Web site at www.envoymagazine.com.

Patrick Madrid's audiotapes and videotapes are available at www.surprisedbytruth.com, (or call 800-234-1161).

Apologetics Workshop: How You Can Become a Master Apologist (three audio tapes).

Catholics and the Rapture: Will You Be Caught Up or Left Behind? (Patrick Madrid and Carl Olson).

The Communion of Saints Debate, Patrick Madrid vs. James White (audiotape, video, CD).

Does the Bible Teach Sola Scriptura? (debate), Patrick Madrid vs. James White.

More Catholic Than the Pope: Why Are Extreme Traditionalists so Extreme? (Patrick Madrid and Peter Vere, J.C.L.).

Radio Apologetics 1, Radio Apologetics 2, Radio Apologetics 3.

Winning Souls, Not Just Arguments (Patrick Madrid and Curtis Martin).

Pope Fiction: Answers to Myths and Misconceptions About the Papacy, Patrick Madrid (sixteen-part EWTN video television series).

ABOUT THE AUTHOR

PATRICK MADRID is an author, public speaker, television host, and the publisher of the award-winning *Envoy* magazine, a journal of Catholic apologetics and evangelization. Its Web site is www.envoymagazine.com.

He is the author of several best-selling books, including *Pope Fiction*, *Where Is That In the Bible?*, *Why Is That In Tradition?*, *Search and Rescue*, *Any Friend of God's Is a Friend of Mine,* and he is the editor and contributor of the acclaimed *Surprised by Truth* series of books (with more than four hundred thousand combined copies in print). He is also the host of three popular EWTN television series: "Pope Fiction," "The Truth About Scripture and Tradition," and "Search and Rescue." He has conducted hundreds of apologetics and evangelization conferences in English and Spanish across the U.S., as well as throughout Europe, Asia, and in Latin America. He is a veteran of numerous formal public debates with Protestant ministers, Mormon leaders, and other non-Catholic spokesmen.

Patrick and his wife, Nancy, have been blessed by God with eleven happy and healthy children. They live in the rolling countryside of Central Ohio. For information about scheduling Patrick Madrid to conduct one of his popular apologetics seminars for your parish or group, please visit his Internet site: www.surprisedbytruth.com, or call 740-587-4881, or e-mail him at patrick@surprisedbytruth.com.